Electro-Horticulture

The Secret to Faster Growth, Larger Yields, and More... Using Electricity!

David J. Wechsler

This book is for sale at http://leanpub.com/ElectricFertilizerBook

This version was published on 2020-03-17

Leanpub

This is a Leanpub book. Leanpub empowers authors and publishers with the Lean Publishing process. Lean Publishing is the act of publishing an in-progress ebook using lightweight tools and many iterations to get reader feedback, pivot until you have the right book and build traction once you do.

© 2012 - 2020 David J. Wechsler

Tweet This Book!

Please help David J. Wechsler by spreading the word about this book on Twitter!

The suggested tweet for this book is:

I just purchased this amazing book on boosting crop yield using electricity! http://ElectricGardeningBook.com #ElectroHorticultureBook

The suggested hashtag for this book is #ElectroHorticultureBook.

Find out what other people are saying about the book by clicking on this link to search for this hashtag on Twitter:

#ElectroHorticultureBook

I dedicate this book to my wife and children for their patience with me in taking the time to research, experiment, and write this book. Thank you!

Contents

Credits i

Preamble 1
   My Story 1
   Purpose of This Book 5
   Potential Benefits of Electroculture 5
   Thank You! 6

Chapter 1: Introduction 7
   Growth Using Electricity? 7

Chapter 2: Electricity & Nature 10
   Electric Agriculture is a Normal Part of Nature 12
   Atmospheric Electricity 12
   Telluric Electricity 19
   Interrelated Energy Systems Working Together 22
   Biological Effects from Natural Electric Phenomena . . . 22
   Summary 24

Chapter 3: The History of Growing with Electricity 25
   18th Century 25
   19th Century 26
   Contemporary Experiments 35
   Summary 38

Chapter 4: The Fundamentals of Soil Science 39
   The Structure of Soil 39

CONTENTS

The Nutrient Cycle 43
Soil Bacteria 47
Summary 48

Chapter 5: Electrical Properties of Soils 49
Electrical Resistivity and Conductivity 50
Summary 56

Chapter 6: Soil Electrochemistry 57
Electric Fields and Soil? 58
Effect on pH 64
Summary 69

Chapter 7: Benefits of Electroculture On Soil 71
Soil Structure 71
Water Capacity 72
Oxygen Content 73
Nutrient Availability 74
Summary 79

Chapter 8: Electroculture And Soil Bacteria 80
Microbial Transport Effects 80
Changes in Metabolic Activity 81
Enhanced Reproductive Activity 83
Stimulation of Aerobic Bacteria 84
Summary 84

Chapter 9: Mechanisms of Plant Electrophysiology 86
Electricity and Polar Cells 88
Electrophysiological Effects 91
Electrical Signaling 98
Electrochemical Signaling 104
Summary 107

Chapter 10: The Effects of Electroculture on Plants 109
Genetic Responses 110

CONTENTS

    Metabolism 113
    Growth Hormones 117
    Increased Number of Roots 120
    Nutrient Uptake Rate 122
    Water Intake 123
    Improved Water Retention 124
    Flowering 127
    Summary 128

Chapter 11: Benefits and Applications 129
    Electro-Tropism 129
    Growth Rate 130
    Improved Fruits and Vegetables Size 134
    Crop Yield 135
    Taste of Fruits and Vegetables 136
    Nutritional Value 137
    Healing Response to Disease 138
    Summary 139

Chapter 12: New Application Ideas 141
    Integrated Pest Management (IPM) 141
    Attraction of Pollinators 143
    Season Extension, Frost and Drought Protection 145
    Rapid Food Growth in Survival, Disaster Response, and
        Quarantine Situations 145
    Accelerated Cleanup of Contaminated Soils 149
    Summary 152

Chapter 13: Try It Yourself! 153
    What You'll Need 153
    Assembly 166
    Installation 175
    System Operation 180
    Summary 181

Chapter 14: Ideas for Further Experimentation 183

CONTENTS

    Questions 183
    Summary 187

Chapter 15: Conclusion 189
    Natural Organic Growth Stimulation 189
    A Vision for the Future of Electroculture 190
    Thank You 193

Appendix: Get Involved 195
    Make Some Discoveries 195

Glossary 196

Bibliography 206

Acknowledgments 222

Special Thanks 223

Credits

I would like to give credit and attribution to all of the researchers, and illustrators as individually noted throughout this book.

Regarding the cover art, I would like to give attribution as follows:

- Design: David Wechsler
- Photo Credits:
- High Yielding Cotton Seedlings[1] / Bishnu Sarangi from Dharwad, India / CC0[2]
- Cucumber[3] / Stephen Ausmus, USDA ARS / Public Domain
- Tomato[4] / Sharon Mollerus from Duluth, USA / CC BY-SA[5]
- Strawberries[6] / Sharon Mollerus from Duluth, USA / CC BY[7]

---

[1] http://pixabay.com/en/bt-cotton-highyielding-seedlings-300916/
[2] http://pixabay.com/go/?t=%2Fservice%2Fterms%2F%23download_terms
[3] http://commons.wikimedia.org/wiki/File:ARS_cucumber.jpg
[4] http://commons.wikimedia.org/wiki/File:Tomato.jpg
[5] http://creativecommons.org/licenses/by-sa/3.0/deed.en
[6] http://commons.m.wikimedia.org/wiki/File:Strawberries_with_hulls_-_scan.jpg
[7] http://creativecommons.org/licenses/by/2.0/deed.en

Preamble

My Story

This book came into being as a result of my curiosity about non-mainstream uses of electricity.

Ever since I was a child, I have been interested in truly alternative forms of science, from the inventions of Nikola Tesla and other high-voltage experimenters to UFOs and science fiction. I loved finding catalogs and books covering esoteric, arcane subjects as well as those that were more normal, but homey. For example, on the esoteric-science side I loved Omni Magazine, and on the science/homey side, I absolutely loved the Whole Earth Catalog[8].

Fast forward to college where I studied electrical engineering and came across a collection of old articles from historical publications ranging from The Scientific American to Popular Science to much older publications that have been out of date for at least a hundred years. In lock-step with my interests in the fantastic and the esoteric, I have also always felt an affinity toward the inventions of the late 1800s. I was completely fascinated by the simple and useful things that were once written about, but were no longer being used. Perhaps they were just experiments that never became popularized, or maybe they became mainstream for a while, only to be crushed out of existence by industrialists of the age.

In time, I found myself most interested in novel, yet simple forms of technology. For example, I have developed a strong interest in "Appropriate Technology," described by Wikipedia[9], as follows:

---

[8] http://www.wholeearth.com/index.php
[9] http://en.wikipedia.org/wiki/Appropriate_technology

> "Appropriate technology is an ideological movement (and its manifestations) originally articulated as "intermediate technology" by the economist Dr. Ernst Friedrich "Fritz" Schumacher in his influential work, *Small is Beautiful*. Though the nuances of appropriate technology vary between fields and applications, it is generally recognized as encompassing technological choice and application that is small scale, labor intensive, energy efficient, environmentally sound and locally controlled."

Very simple ideas can be used worldwide to help people with food production, sanitation, energy, food storage and more. Well-known examples of appropriate technology include:

- Bike-, hand-, and other self-powered forms of pumps
- Self-contained solar-powered lamps and street lights
- Passive solar building designs

All of these interests came together for me when I discovered the topic of electrifying plants. When I was in high school, my father helped me put together a Van De Graaff Generator[10] and I was always experimenting with it. In some old articles describing high-voltage electrostatics, I came across some materials about using electricity for growing plants. This field of study had a name: Electroculture.

From the late 1800s to the early 1930s, the field exploded, with a surge of experimentation, articles and books, but after a period of controversy in the early 1920s, most of the information withered away except for a few traces here and there. Since then, research just slightly picked up during the '60s, '70s and '80s, with some new research from 2000 to the present.

---

[10]http://en.wikipedia.org/wiki/Van_de_Graaff_generator

After reading about the ways these researchers were able to achieve fantastic results by electrifying their plants in various ways, I decided to try an experiment on my own.

It was February 2011, and I decided to experiment with Romanesco broccoli by doing a side-by-side comparison. For this first electrification experiment, I turned a plastic lettuce container into a makeshift pot, and planted some seeds in it. The others I planted in typical fashion, in 2-inch cell pots. Both sets of plants were grown under the exact same conditions, including soil, light, heat, and ventilation, but the first set of plants was electrified.

Although I was completely skeptical about the project, I was absolutely surprised when after one week I saw results! The electrified group of plants had stalks that were twice as long as the non-electrified group.

Figure 1: Results of my 1st Electroculture Experiment (control on left / electrified on right)

After one month, the differences between the two sets of plants were astonishing! The experimental group had leaves that were almost twice as wide as the other, and the color of the entire group of electrified plants was a lush, deep, rainforest-green compared to the medium-green look of the non-electrified set of plants.

Later on, the growth was even more pronounced, with the electrified plants towering over the control group.

1.5 Months Afterwards... See the electrified ones towering over everything else!

Please excuse my poor staging / picture taking abilities :)

The experiment turned out to be a great success! These initial results and my continuing success in growing plants with electricity - far exceeding my expectations - has propelled me into deep study of the subject and the creation of this book.

Purpose of This Book

The purpose of this book is to show how direct-current electric fields can be applied to plants and soils to greatly increase the health, vitality, and productivity of plants - safely, cost-effectively and sustainably. One of my goals is teaching the latest research on the subject and sharing what I have learned along the way, which includes answering some of the questions that I commonly hear, e.g.:

- Is this for real?
- How does it work?
- Has it ever been studied or researched?
- Are there any formal scientific studies?

Another goal is to inspire readers to try experiments on their own, perhaps on plants that aren't mentioned in any of the studies described in this book - and to become part of a discovery effort for the benefit of all. As you read this book, you will see that although there are many known mechanisms at work, there is much more that is unknown. Much more research and exploration is needed in this field to fully understand what is going on and to achieve the full potential of the technology.

Potential Benefits of Electroculture

Electroculture, also known as electro-horticulture, holds great promise for helping to solve many of our culture's pressing needs. I envision these techniques to be most useful for the following:

- **Fighting disease.** Helping farmers throughout the world who are fighting against enormous losses due to pathogens and

disease. This technology can help combat many plant diseases without using any chemicals or antibiotics.
- **Reducing risk from weather volatility.** Due to the volatile weather patterns that can greatly affect crop growth: early frosts, storm damage, flooding, droughts and other conditions, huge crop losses occur annually. If these techniques could increase the growth rate of plants and allow farmers to harvest their crops ahead of schedule, thus mitigating many of the random risks that could occur, the savings can be substantial!
- **Improving profits & saving money.** For small and large scale growers alike who are making a living off of their land, using these methods can potentially boost their yields up to 200 percent or more, resulting in much greater profits without the use of expensive fertilizers (or possibly insecticides, too).

Thank You!

I hope you enjoy this book and that it helps spread the virtues of electric agriculture.

- David Wechsler, Author & Founder of ElectricFertilizer.com[11]

---
[11] https://ElectricFertilizer.com/

Chapter 1: Introduction

Did you know there is a technology capable of helping plants grow more than twice as fast as usual? Capable of more than doubling the yields of crops? That can cure, in minutes, diseases normally considered incurable?

Is this science fiction? A brand new technology? No. These results are very possible and very real. The technology exists and, in fact, isn't new technology at all.

For centuries, enterprising farmers have looked for ways to make plants grow better and faster. Most research has been plant-based and focused on nutrients and farming methods, ranging from land-based methods, like crop rotation and the use of specialized synthetic fertilizers, to more specialized methods like hydroponics and aeroponics. Another technology, though, has been around for more than 200 years and has been very successful in helping plants grow faster, with higher yields, better health, stronger disease resistance and more.

This technology is simply the use of pure electricity, the same stuff that powers your cell phones and mp3 players!

Growth Using Electricity?

Electricity is a Normal Part of Growth & Development

Most people know that the human body has electrical components within the nervous system, but did you know that electricity can be found nearly everywhere? Many kinds of electrical signals exist in animals and plants too. In animals and humans, electricity regulates neural signals that control bodily functions like heart rate, muscle movement and brain activity. Plants, like animals, are also electric organisms. In plants, neural signals known as action potentials are present in stimulus–response mechanisms, like that of the Venus Fly Trap. When triggered by its sense of touch, electrochemical messages are transmitted that cause the plant to trap its insect prey. Other types of electrical response mechanisms that are present in both plants and animals are via the electrochemical movement of atoms and complex molecules into and out-of cells. These building-blocks, both simple and complex, often have an electrical charge associated with them, and thus can be transported into and out-of cellular structures by manipulating the charge of various gateways within the cell-wall. Electricity is an intrinsic part of life.

Consider how life responds to electrical energy. Modern medicine uses electricity in many different ways, from helping wounds heal faster to jump-starting a heart. In the plant world, there is a growing body of research that suggests that plants respond favorably to the high-voltage static electric fields that are generated by thunderstorms. Other studies show that under the influence of an electrical field, seeds may experience both an increase in fertility and improved disease resistance response, ultimately resulting in an increased germination rate.

In fact, a number of electrical systems are a part of the Earth itself. These range from the Van Allen radiation belts[12] that protect the planet from cosmic radiation, to the energy contained in lightning storms, to the natural geomagnetism that influences our navigational compasses. Natural electric currents called telluric currents even move through the crust of the earth, playing a part in all of life that we don't fully understand. In many ways, electrical energy plays a planetary-wide role that promotes and supports life itself.

Given this understanding of electricity as an intrinsically benevolent part of life, what do you think would happen if electricity was

---

[12] http://en.wikipedia.org/wiki/Van_Allen_radiation_belt

applied in an engineered manner? Can we do better?

Boosted Development with Electricity

Scientists for as long as 200 years have observed amazing results in boosting healthy plant growth and deterring disease by directly applying various forms of electricity to soil. Known most commonly as electroculture, these methods are the subject of this book. Other terms describing the use of electricity to help plants grow include electro-horticulture, electro-therapy, and the plant electro-physiology.

In this book you will learn how to access the electricity's power of improving plant growth by exploring the following:

- Many validating experiments, both old and new.
- Scientific background material needed to more fully understand the processes involved.
- The effects of electro-tropism on plants, soils and bacteria.
- Experiments you can try to further your knowledge and contribute via the building up of global knowledge available on the subject.

In the next chapter, we look at centuries-old experiments that provide some proof of the effectiveness of these techniques and point the way for continued research.

Chapter 2: Electricity & Nature

The fabric of all things in physical form on this planet is based on an elemental atomic structure. Biological entities are composed of interconnected cellular structures forming tissues, organs and biochemical networks. At the core are atomic elements, each of which is associated with some level of electrical charge. These charges are the basis for the forces of electrochemical attraction and repulsion that occur within the cellular structures of all living things.

> **Electrostatic (or electro-chemical) attraction and repulsion**, is based on a fundamental property of matter that have opposing or similar electric charges. Atoms, molecules, and other complex structures can have a composition differing amounts of electrical charge, both positive and negative. When two or more substances are next to each other with differing charges, i.e. a positive and a negative, the negative is attracted to the positive and the positive is attracted to the negative. When they are the same, positively charged substances are repelled from other positively charged substances. The same goes for negatively charged substances.

Like-charges repel

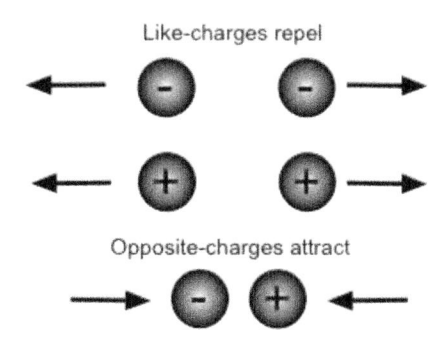

Opposite-charges attract

Electrostatic Attraction and Repulsion

The interactions between these components are vast, making use of many forms of information and electro-biological mechanisms. This includes electro-chemistry, biophysics, genetics and perhaps other forms of study that are beyond our current understanding. An example of this would be the study of subtle energies, bio-energetics and quantum physics, which are in many ways still in their infancy.

> For example, not only are large molecules such as proteins usually electrically charged, but did you know that DNA itself is also highly charged? It is these electrostatic forces that hold the molecule together and give it structure and strength.[a]
>
> [a] Electric Forces in Biology

Electric Agriculture is a Normal Part of Nature

Now that we know that electrically-based particles and forces are present within all of life, is it too far-fetched to state that electrical forces are not only intrinsic to life, but are necessary to thrive?

We will begin by covering the natural occurrences of electromagnetic fields within the atmosphere, followed by the presence of natural electrical currents that are continuously flowing throughout the surface of the Earth. Lastly, we'll touch on how these electro-geological systems impact life in various ways.

Atmospheric Electricity

Flashes, booms and brilliant light shows were the earliest evidence that electricity is a naturally powerful force, intrinsically available to humanity. From the legend of Benjamin Franklin and his 1752 kite-flying experiment[13], his discovery of the presence and subsequent capture of atmospheric electricity set the stage for centuries' worth of scientific exploration, discovery and engineering.

---

[13] http://en.wikipedia.org/wiki/Kite_experiment

Lightning Storm

Source: Boby Dimitrov[14]

There are between 2,000 and 6,000 thunderstorms in progress at any one time, on any given day, all over the Earth. As such, at any one time, there is an enormous amount of electricity located throughout the skies. So, on an average day, how much electricity is actually swirling around us?

It has been determined through many measurements that the average fair-weather electric field is approximately 100 to 300 Volts per meter at the surface of the Earth. Of course, these values are constantly changing. This is due to a number of factors that include day-night cycles, seasonal cycles, as well as upper atmosphere and space-based cycles and events. Thus if we were to take into consideration the amount of space between the surface of the Earth and the outer edge of the Earth's atmosphere, the ionosphere, we would see that the average voltage present across that region would be approximately 360,000 Volts at any one time. As we come down from these high altitudes, the electric field diminishes in strength. At sea-level, this ends up being approximately 100 Volts per meter[15]. What this means is that at any given moment, the air all around us is filled with lots of electrical energy!

---
[14] https://www.flickr.com/photos/63465428@N00/3701793926/
[15] (McDonald, 1953)

Ionosphere

**60 miles
360,000 Volts**

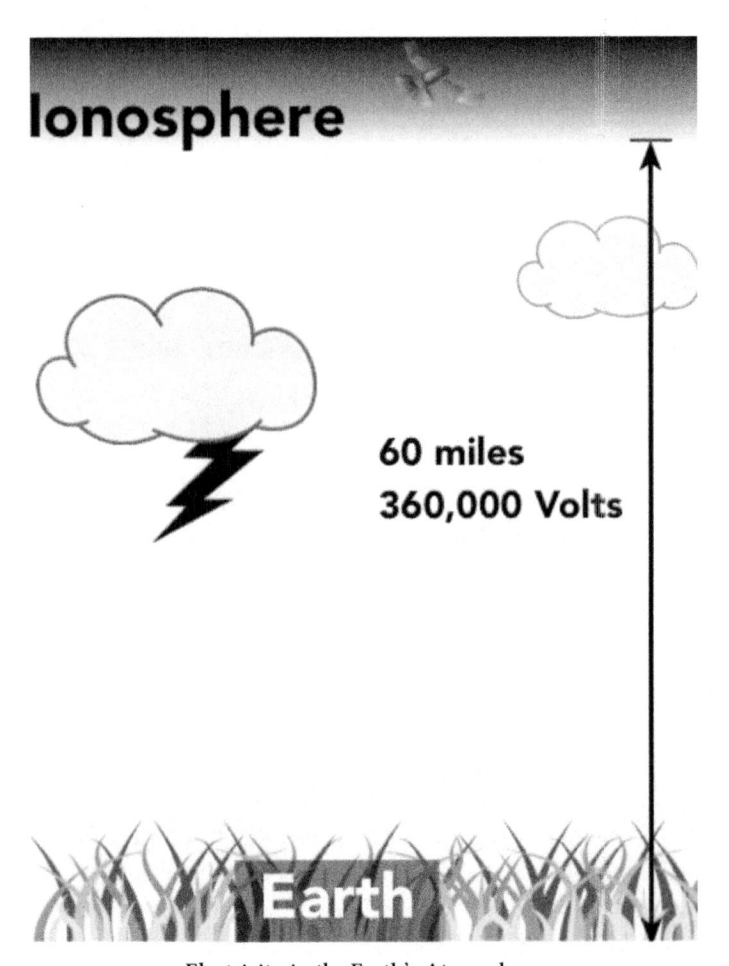

Earth

Electricity in the Earth's Atmosphere

Lightning Storms

Later on in the chapter we're going to learn that plants require exposure to naturally-occurring electric fields in order to survive. In the meantime, let's see how plants respond when they're subjected to naturally-occurring additional amounts of electricity.

Chapter 2: Electricity & Nature   15

In his book, *Blinded By Science*, Matthew Silverstone informs us that plants can detect when a thunderstorm is on the way. Plant physiologist Andrew Goldsworthy[16], suspects that in anticipation of a change in weather, they increase their growth rate so they can increase their capacity for water absorption. Not knowing when their next drink is going to come available, they cleverly grow a little more before the arrival of the rains so they can "gorge on the extra water available."[17]

In the study of Paleolightning[18], it is speculated that lightning played a part in the genesis of early life. Further studies on the subject have found that lightning storms improve nitrogen fixation, boosting the development of plant life[19]. Yet, there may be other factors at play, according to the research of L.E. Murr who wrote about the stimulation effect of plants in electrostatic fields[20].

What's interesting is that there have been many reports over the ages stating that plants generally look healthier after a thunderstorm. As an example, one time in late 2013 on GardenWeb, a man named Derek said, "When it rains, all of my plants grow a lot more than with just plain old watering in the morning. It's rained for about 3 days on and off here with some sunshine and my pumpkin vines have easily grown 6 inches but it will take a week for them to grow that much with no rain and just water?"[21]

Most experts state that the primary reason for this effect is that lightning turns atmospheric nitrogen into a form (nitrous oxide) more easily assimilated by plants. So when nitrogen-enriched rain falls from the skies, it gives them a boost.

My hypothesis, based on information found in Chapters 9 and 10, is that under the conditions of an electrical storm, the abundance of free-floating ions in the air creates a charge imbalance on plant

---
[16] (Goldsworthy, 2006)
[17] (Silverstone, 2011)
[18] http://en.wikipedia.org/wiki/Paleolightning
[19] (Uman, 1996)
[20] The biophysics of plant growth in a reversed electrostatic field
[21] GardenWeb

cell walls. As you will see, this imbalance will lead to a wide array of physiological changes.

Other forms of atmospheric electricity that have also been found to be beneficial to plant life include the high-latitude display of the Aurora Borealis and the bombardment of the Earth by cosmic radiation.

Aurora Borealis

Aurora Borealis: High-Energy Atmospheric Lightshows

Source: Jerry Magnum Porsbjer[22]

According to Professor Selim Lemström's experimental work in 1904[23], electrical fields from the Aurora Borealis are responsible for green and healthy vegetation in the Arctic. Since the effect is related to a large amounts of electric charge being present in the upper-atmosphere, this may be true. Here's an explanation of the

---

[22]http://en.wikipedia.org/wiki/File:Northern_light_01.jpg
[23](Lemström, 1904)

mechanics behind the lights by way of the Tromsø Geophysical Observatory at University of Tromsø in Norway:

"The northern lights originate in a complicated interplay between the so-called solar wind and the earth's magnetic field. The solar wind is a constant stream of electric particles from the sun. It varies in intensity and therefore links the northern lights with the solar activity. The solar winds rushes along the earth's magnetic field, compresses it on the day side, draws it out into a tail on the night side and generates electric currents and fields in the areas around the earth. A number of solar wind particles are trapped in the earth's magnetic field and, together with particles which originate in the earth's atmosphere, end up in the tail on the magnetic field on the night side. As a result of mechanisms we still do not really understand, they receive extra energy there, stream toward the polar regions at great speed and give us the night-time aurora. These unpredictable showers of electric particles controlled by the earth's magnetic field give the northern lights their forms and movements."

As an example of the land-based effects of these strong electromagnetic fields, consider the following sampling of old telegraph reports from 1851 and 1852[24]:

---

[24]The Atlantic Monthly, December 1859, p. 744-745

"It is in the United States, however, that the action of the aurora upon the telegraph wires was the most remarkable. A fantastic aurora occurred in September of 1851. This took complete possession of all the telegraph lines in New England and prevented any business from being transacted during its duration. The following winter, on February 19, 1852, another aurora left its mark in history. On this date, the system of telegraphing used upon the wires was Bain's chemical. No batteries were kept constantly upon the line, as in the Morse and other magnetic systems. The main wire was connected directly with the chemically prepared paper on the disc so that any atmospheric currents were recorded with the greatest accuracy. The usual battery current, decomposing the salts in the paper and uniting with the iron point of the pen-wire, left a light blue mark on the white paper. Or, if the current were strong, a dark blue mark would be left on the paper. The color of the mark depended upon the quantity of the current upon the wire."

The following is an actual account from the journal of an electric telegrapher:

Thursday, February 19, 1852

"Towards evening, a heavy blue line appeared upon the paper, which gradually increased in size for the space of half a minute, when a flame of fire succeeded to the blue line, of sufficient intensity to burn through a dozen thicknesses of the moistened paper. The current then subsided as gradually as it had come on, until it entirely ceased, and was then succeeded by a negative current (which bleaches, instead of coloring, the paper). This gradually increased, in the same manner as the positive current, until it also, in turn, produced its flame of fire, and burned through many thicknesses of the prepared paper; it then subsided, again to be followed by the positive current. This state of things continued during the entire evening, and effectually prevented any business being done over the wires."

While I haven't yet found any studies that show a correlation between arctic crop yields and Aurora Borealis, I think that if any studies were performed, they would be beneficial for testing the Lemström's hypotheses. It would then be exciting to show cold-climate farmers that the Earth naturally boosts crop production to make up for very short growing seasons.

Telluric Electricity

In roughly the same time period that experiments with atmospheric electricity began, another discovery was made: the Earth (i.e. the ground) itself is electrically active!

In the early 1860s, scientists around the world were experimenting with earth-based electrical systems in the form of "Earth batteries". In 1862, one scientist[25] from the Munich Alps performed an experiment that revealed to the world that natural electric fields exist within the Earth!

In this experiment, two metal plates were placed, some distance apart, into the ground along the Earth's magnetic or astronomical meridians, i.e. North-South lines. They were then connected together using some wire along with a sensitive voltmeter or ammeter. What was observed was the presence of natural forms of electricity that were generally stronger in the North-South direction compared to the East-West directions. In fact, it was discovered that the strongest currents flowed South to North.

Upon further experimentation, the following additional observations were made. The currents:

- Flow on the surface of the Earth
- Follow a path of least resistance
- Move between each hemisphere constantly

[25](Lamont, 1862)

Chapter 2: Electricity & Nature   20

- Move differently in the day and the night:
- Daytime: Currents move toward the equator
- Nighttime: Currents move toward the poles

Furthermore, by taking measurements in many different places, maps could be created showing the relative strengths of these fields over certain geographic areas.

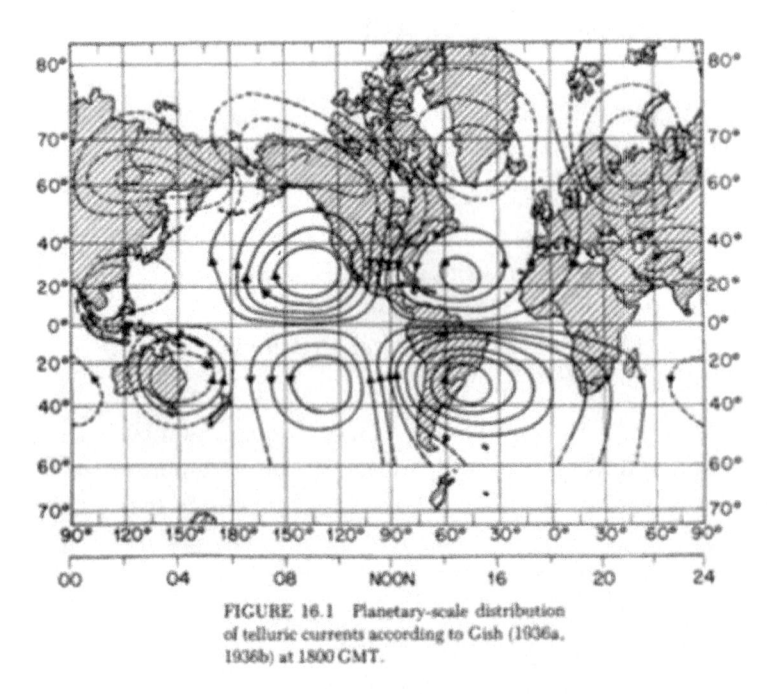

FIGURE 16.1 Planetary-scale distribution of telluric currents according to Gish (1936a, 1936b) at 1800 GMT.

A 1936 Map of Telluric Electrical Currents

Source: (Gish, 1936)

Cosmic and Planetary Influences

So where do Earth-currents come from?

A good portion of these "induced" electric fields over the planet come from interactions between the solar wind and the magnetosphere. From what we know so far, the Van Allen belts and the magnetosphere are what protects the surface against harmful cosmic radiation. They are also the result of interactions between the sun's radiation and the planet's ionosphere. Variations in these bodies range from subtle changes over days or weeks to rapidly changing geomagnetic "storms." These storms are capable of inducing varying amounts of electricity in the ground [26]. Thus, along with shifts in the electromagnetic activity of our atmosphere and space weather, the Earth is also affected in some way.

An excellent resource on the subject of atmospheric and telluric electricity can be found in a collection of articles called "The Earth's Electrical Environment"[27].

It's worth noting that there has been some interesting research regarding the presence of abnormally-high electro-magnetic fields being present at a number of "sacred sites" around the world. Sites ranging from Stonehenge in the UK to Monk's Mound in Cahokia, Illinois have been found to exhibit large peaks in electric field strength at certain times of the day. Check out some of the following resources to learn more:

- *Places of Power: Measuring the Secret Energy of Ancient Sites* by Paul Devereux[28]
- *Seed of Knowledge, Stone of Plenty: Understanding the Lost Technology of the Ancient Megalith-Builders* by John Burke

---

[26] (Lanzerotti et al., 1986)
[27] http://www.nap.edu/catalog.php?record_id=898
[28] http://www.pauldevereux.co.uk/

Interrelated Energy Systems Working Together

As you can imagine, the interactions between geophysical and cosmic energies are quite complex, and still not completely understood. What's interesting is that these interactions may not be completely random. Surely they could be, but perhaps these systems are really a part of a cosmo-planetary communication system that links together solar influences, including that of the moon, to astrological influences, to planetary energies as well. The system is obviously very complex, and thus beautiful to ponder... so much to understand and discover!

Biological Effects from Natural Electric Phenomena

So what are the biological effects that come from the intersection between these cosmo-planetary energies and biology? Let's look at a few case studies:

Electric Fields and Plant Life

Since we now understand that the air around us is naturally charged, we can form a hypothesis that states that plants (and perhaps all surface life as well) require exposure to electric fields in order to grow properly. This idea has been tested a number of times throughout history.

Supporting this are a few studies that have shown that plants can have a difficult time surviving when grown under a form of electromagnetic shielding known as a Faraday's Cage[29].

---

[29] http://en.wikipedia.org/wiki/Faraday_cage

One early experiment was performed in 1898 by M. Grandeau, a French agricultural chemist, and M. Leclerq who performed studies into the effect of atmospheric electricity on plants. They discovered that shielding plants from the Earth's naturally-present electric field using a grounded wire net had a detrimental effect on plant health, stating that the plants looked "feebly"[30]. It turned out that the uncovered plants grew 50 to 60 percent better than the shielded plants. Furthermore, they found that flowering and fruiting processes were also adversely affected.[31] [32] [33]

This has been studied in modern times too. Here's an example from Steven Magee[34] on YouTube[35] that shows how plants suffer a loss of chlorophyll content and other abnormalities when placed in a wire cage. In this video, you'll see how a houseplant is adversely affected by the lack of atmospheric electricity, as demonstrated by its nearly transparent, discolored, smaller and somewhat deformed leaves.

Now that we can experimentally see that exposure to electric fields is essential, we can also see that researchers have found other examples showing the coupling of biology to electro-magnetic forces:

- Magnetic fields have been discovered as being used for the

---

[30]Electricity: A Popular Electrical Journal, Volumes 4-5, Electricity Newspaper Company, 1893

[31](Nature, 1879)

[32](Artem, 2012)

[33]On the other hand, in (Nature, 1879), there is a data point showing that M. Naudin found the opposite to be true. In his experiments, he claims that his plants flourished when placed under an electrical cage. Per my understanding, I can attribute the differences to a number of things. First, as you will see later on, plants respond to stimuli on a species-to-species basis - what's effective for one type of plant isn't necessarily effective for another. Second, since the details of Grandeau's and Leclerq's experiments are not available, it's not possible to make an "apples to apples" comparison. Because Naudin experienced a boost in output, I would posit that his cage was actually leaky. I also suspect that his cage accumulated charge for the plant's benefit via metal points located on the tops of his cage. To really test this out, someone would need to perform a three-way experiment to see how both fare against the control group.

[34]Steven Magee is a researcher interested in the harmful effects of high-frequency electro-magnetic RF radiation.

[35]https://www.youtube.com/watch?v=Ia_6ipxxeAs

orientation of aquatic bacteria[36] and migrating birds[37].
- Telluric currents could play a role in the control of some fish.[38]
- Enhanced DNA synthesis has been reported for human fibroblasts exposed to magnetic field fluctuations that correlate with frequencies and amplitudes similar to geomagnetic occurrences.[39]
- Weak magnetic fields (e.g. those from solar storms or geomagnetic fields) may affect how chemical reactions perform.[40]
- And, as will be covered throughout the rest of the book, plants react to electric fields through faster growth, greener leaves and stems, increased root mass and more!

Summary

Since we now know that extremely low levels of various forms of energy are required for (plant) life to simply survive, and we also know that there have been times that life seems to flourish when there is an abundance of electrical energy present, the next step is to figure out how we can develop engineered methods to optimize growth processes at our own discretion, rather than hoping for a few passing thunderstorms to enhance crop growth.

In the next chapter we'll start with learning about electroculture in a historical context, seeing what experimenters have been able to achieve through the deliberate electrification of plants and soils.

---

[36](Blakemore, 1975) via The Earth's Electrical Environment, Chapter 16
[37](Moore, 1977; Larkin and Sutherland, 1977; Alerstam and Högstedt, 1983; Beason and Nichols, 1984) via The Earth's Electrical Environment, Chapter 16
[38](e.g., Leggett, 1977; Kalmijn, 1978; Brown et al., 1979; Fainberg, 1980; Fonarev, 1982) via The Earth's Electrical Environment, Chapter 16
[39](Li- et al., 1984) via The Earth's Electrical Environment, Chapter 16
[40](Agulova, L.P. and A.M, Opalinskaya, 1990)

Chapter 3: The History of Growing with Electricity

In North America, approximately thirty years before the signing of the Declaration of Independence, at a time when the discovery and use of electricity was in its infancy, experimenters in England were already exploring the effects of electricity upon plant life[41]. The effects were so pronounced that other researchers joined the effort, propelling the movement forward.

Electroculture, as it is known today, is the use of electrical current to stimulate the growth of plants. While the term is relatively new, the concept is not. There were hundreds of researchers working in the field between the years of 1745 and 1910, and even more researchers working from 1918 to 1936[42], when it was at its peak in terms of popularity. Today, researchers are again studying the phenomena.

Here is a brief look at its early experimental history...

18th Century

In 1746, a researcher named Dr. Von Maimbray of Edinburgh, Scotland, conducted experiments to discover what effects electricity might have on plant life. His first experiment, performed on two young myrtle trees, consisted of simply passing a current through the trees to the earth using static electricity. To his surprise, the growth of the trees was significantly stimulated, showing greater growth in both the leaves as well as the height of the main

---
[41](Hull, 1898)
[42](Hull, 1898)

trunk. Consequently he declared that some sort of "electric fluid" increased the rate of growth in plants[43].

Through the years other researchers joined him. They used various methods produced similar results, showing that plants can receive enormous benefits when "fertilized" with electricity. Still more researchers joined the ranks...

19th Century

It wasn't until the mid-1800s that further experimentation on plants began to take off. The increase in interest was due to the invention of what was called an "Earth battery[44]." Invented[45] by Alexander Bain in 1841, the earth battery generated electrical power by placing plates of zinc and copper, connected by a wire above the ground, into the earth. When plants were placed into the ground between the plates, an increase in both growth rate and yield would often be observed. It's essentially based on the same principles as common batteries today, but instead of being designed to fit into a tiny space inside our cars, boats and consumer electronic devices, it operates in dirt over distances ranging from inches to hundreds of feet!

---

[43] (Hull, 1898)
[44] http://en.wikipedia.org/wiki/Earth_battery
[45] More likely, re-discovered.

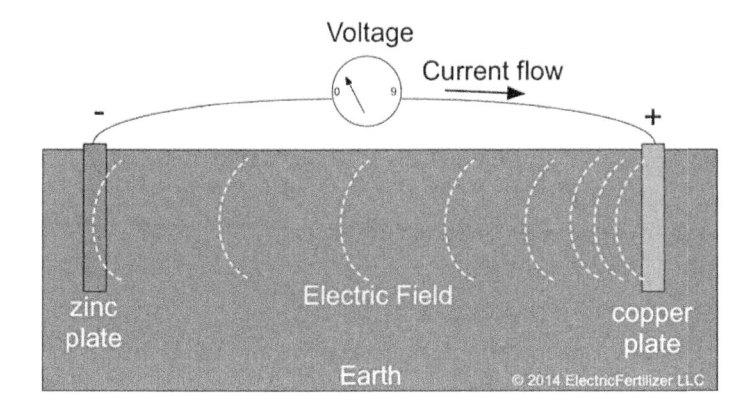

Chapter 3: The History of Growing with Electricity 27

Earth Battery

An 'Earth' Battery In Your Kitchen...

An earth battery works just like a lemon-powered clock, the kind used in educational settings to demonstrate that electricity can come from almost anywhere. A lemon (or potato or tomato) is often used as the medium, and a digital clock is plugged into it. The thing is, it's really a trick. These types of clocks aren't actually powered by the fruits or vegetables that they plug into; instead, the electrical energy that's delivered comes from the metal electrodes that are plugged into the fruit or vegetable. In simple terms, the differences in electrical potential innate to the materials of zinc and copper (the electrodes used in these devices) actually powers the clock. The electrically-conductive innards of the lemons, potatoes or tomatoes are used as a catalyst, creating the conditions needed for electricity to flow between the two different metals. For more information, look up the Lemon Battery[a] in Wikipedia.

[a] http://en.wikipedia.org/wiki/Lemon_battery

An agriculturist named Ross was described in the *Proceedings of the New York Farmers' Club*, a publication from the 1850s, using an earth battery system in some experiments. In one performed in 1844, he used a copper plate that was 5 feet by 14 inches, connected to a zinc plate of the same dimensions, placing them 200 feet apart at opposite ends of a row of potatoes. When the potatoes were harvested from the electrified row, they were five times larger in diameter than other potatoes grown at the same time in fields that weren't electrified[46].

Once the discovery of an inexpensive way to generate electricity in the ground was made, and the beneficial effects of growing within this "battery" were demonstrated, interest in this idea grew. Many of the records from the late 1700s to the 1930s show people experimenting with earth batteries and their effects on plants.

Sir H. Davy, a British chemist and inventor, found that seeds placed closer to the positive electrode of an earth battery germinated faster than those placed closer to the negative pole (he attributed this effect to the fact that the positive pole generates oxygen underneath the soil). He also ran several experiments on barley, wheat, rye, radishes, turnips, and others and found that plants exposed to even a minimal amount of electrical stimulation achieved greater growth than those that weren't electrified[47].

However, not all of the early electroculture experiments achieved positive results. Experimenters named Helmert and Wollny performed experiments where the resulting crops were weaker and others where the crops even died[48]. Many unaccounted-for variables could have been the cause of the failures and, without detailed observations, and soil analyses, it would be difficult to determine the reasons some experiments failed while others flourished.

A lack of detailed measurements, as well as crude experimental methods led to much early criticism. In some cases not enough plants were measured to make up a substantial sample size. In any

---

[46]Cyclopedia
[47]Solly, 1845
[48]Briggs, et. al., 1926

Chapter 3: The History of Growing with Electricity   29

case, researchers have determined that this method doesn't work equally well with all plants, and this discovery may have led to a downturn of interest in this field.

However, there were many more successes than failures. Here are some examples of these early successes from the *Cyclopedia of American Agriculture*:

- A grower by the name of Fitchner demonstrated very positive results from growing buckwheat, summer wheat, peas and other crops with yield increases of 16 to 127 percent.
- Sheppard in 1846 used copper and zinc plates 2 feet long and 9 inches wide, 9 feet apart for his earth battery experiments. Many plants germinated poorly, except for turnips which did better than those in his control group.
- Blondeau found that when seeds of peas, beans and wheat were electrified for one minute, germination was hastened, and stockier, greener plants resulted. He also found that when electricity was applied to fruit trees such as apple and pear, the fruit ripened much earlier.
- McLoud found that with the use of electricity many seeds germinated earlier and also experienced larger growth compared to untreated seeds.
- In 1896 a researcher named Kinney ran a series of experiments with small currents ranging from 0.05 to 1 milliamp applied to lettuce and radishes. He achieved growth rates averaging 34 to 37 percent greater than the control.
- George Hull, an author from California, used an earth battery "in a box" to replicate some of the experiments performed by earlier researchers (See box below for details).

Chapter 3: The History of Growing with Electricity 30

An Old Electroculture Experiment

Source: Häntzschel, Walter, *The influence of electricity on plant growth*(Ref)[49]

---

[49]http://de.m.wikipedia.org/wiki/Elektrokultur#

Chapter 3: The History of Growing with Electricity   31

> In one experiment he planted hemp seeds in two boxes. One box had a thin piece of zinc the same width and depth of the box, pressed almost to the bottom of the box. On the other side of the box was a copper plate of similar size, which was connected to the zinc plate via a copper wire running on top. The use of zinc as one terminal led it to become the positively charged terminal, and the copper subsequently became the negative terminal. He saw increases in plant growth of 20 to 40 percent, which he attributed to the current flow present in the soil. This was measured using a sensitive electrical current meter (known as an ammeter). Note: He could have used a chemical battery (available at the time) for his experiment, but the earth battery was significantly less expensive.

Many French scientists, including Barat of Aiguillon from Lot-et-Garonne in southern France, experimented with the electrical stimulation of plants since 1880. Among Barat's best results were the following:

- A row of hemp that was intermittently under the influence of electrical current ended up with stalks 18 inches taller than those grown in another row under similar conditions but without electricity.
- A kilo of seed potatoes in an electrified patch produced 21 kg of large, well-conditioned tubers while the non-electrified potato patch produced only 12.4 kg of tubers that were far less healthy and smaller in size, a gain of 69%!
- Fruit ripened as much as eight days earlier on trees that were treated with an electric current[50].

Around 1886, Speschnew, a Russian agriculturalist, was working

---
[50](Electrician, 1892)

in the Royal Botanical Gardens in Kew, London. He used an earth battery system to attain the following results[51]:

- Vegetable stalks four times larger than normal.
- Grain yield 50 percent greater than normal.
- Radishes 17 inches long and 5 inches in diameter.
- A carrot 11 inches in diameter and weighing almost five pounds.
- Both the radishes and the carrots were juicy and tasted great.
- On the germination of seeds, he determined that the application of bursts of electrical current onto seeds accelerated germination by 20 percent. He further claimed that it increased the vitality of the germ, which he demonstrated by successfully germinating very old seeds[52].

A fantastic discovery came about from a person named Fischer from the Waldstein mountains in Bavaria, Germany, who experimented with garden plants using an earth battery with plates 65 by 40 centimeters in the soil, 30 meters (90 feet) apart. Using this method, he achieved crops with faster growth and increases of 200 to 400 percent in yield for certain types of plants(it would be nice if we knew which ones). He also came to the same conclusion as Speschnew in demonstrating that his plants were predominantly free from disease by conducting experiments that were in environments where the surrounding plants were badly affected by fungi[53].

An Old Electroculture Experiment

---

[51](Hull, 1898)
[52]*Gardener's Chronicle*
[53](Hull, 1898)

Chapter 3: The History of Growing with Electricity

Source: Häntzschel, Walter, *The influence of electricity on plant growth*(Ref)[54]

In a different type of experiment that was verified at the Hatch Experiment Station in Amherst, MA[55], Professor Warner of the Agricultural College of Massachusetts in 1897 replicated the results of European researchers and discovered some new results of his own. In one greenhouse, in which lettuce was severely affected by mildew, he ran an experiment to see if electricity would be a useful form of treatment. He sowed head lettuce over two sets of stranded wires, one set containing four strands and another nine strands, each strand being half an inch apart. Two standard batteries generated a current of electricity through the wires.

The following chart show the results of that experiment.

	Survived	Diseased or Died
Electrically-Stimulated Group (15 sowed)	10 (developed into large heads)	5 (died)
Control Group (15 sowed)	1 (healthy)	2 (nearly destroyed) 12 (died)

Prof Warner's Results - Lettuce Experiment

Interestingly enough, Warner found that the largest heads of lettuce were the ones over the largest bundle of wires and closest to the battery terminal. He also discovered a high density of roots around the wires "as if they found maximum nourishment around the wires." When the current became weak or was interrupted, likely due to the soil becoming dry, the lettuce heads began to be affected by the mildew. This conclusion was the same as Fischer's, with respect to showing that plants badly affected by fungi can be protected. He also observed the following:

[54]http://de.m.wikipedia.org/wiki/Elektrokultur#
[55]Its name has since been changed to the Massachusetts Agricultural Experiment Station

- The lettuce heads in his experiment were generally hardier, healthier, had better color and were much less affected by the mildew than the lettuce in the control group.
- In similar experiments performed later, parsnips, salsify (*Tragopogon porrifolius*), radishes and peas thrived.
- Turnips and beets responded to a lesser degree.

It's worth noting that this particular experiment differs from most of the other ones in that the force that most likely had an effect was the induced presence of a fixed magnetic field. But since we don't know whether the wires were insulated or not, it is tough to say.

George Truffault, a follower of the research of Von Maimbray and Barat, wrote an article entitled "Electricity Controls Tree Growth" for the August 1935 issue of *Popular Science*. In it, he describes his ability to either boost, or stunt, the growth of fruit trees in his orchard by applying electrical fields[56].

Knowing that tree crops can also benefit from this technology has many positive implications. For example, by accelerating the growth of citrus trees, the growers of these crops could protect themselves against early frosts through earlier harvests.

In addition to all of the experiments performed by individual agricultural scientists and experimenters, in the 1920s, the United States and United Kingdom both formed government commissions to investigate the effects of electricity on plant growth. In the U.K., large-scale field trials on oats by the Ministry of Agriculture and Fisheries (MAF) Committee in 1920 reported increases in yield by 30 to 50 percent[57], but as time went on, a series of crop failures occurred that eventually caused the shutting-down of the organizations. While some suppose that the disbanding was mostly due to a series of adverse weather conditions, a number of other reasons may be the true cause of crop failure and organizational failure as well. As for the crop failures, while a series of droughts

---
[56](Popular Science, 1935)
[57](Chopra)

for an extended period of time would certainly be one issue, another would be the lack of understanding regarding the long-term effects of earth battery-based stimulation[58], which was the primary method used at the time. The other issue that may have affected the organization as a whole was the growing influence of the synthetic fertilizer industry, which may have seen the practice of electroculture as a threat.[59]

Contemporary Experiments

It seems that every 20 years or so a resurgence of experimentation with this form of agriculture occurs.

J.D. Black et al., in a 1971 edition of the *Canadian Journal of Botany*, showed that the rate of linear growth of tomato plants could be stimulated by various amounts in the range of 5 to 30 percent by passing a small current between the plant and the soil[60].

L. E. Murr, one of the most active researchers of the 1960s and 1970s, conducted a series of experiments in the electrification of plants and obtained the following primary results into the reason why it worked:

- Increased metabolic activity
- Increased density of chloroplasts

His experiments also showed that beneficial plant growth could be stimulated through the use of very low strength magnetic fields and that an increase in weight of sweet corn could be obtained through the use of a wide range of electric field stimulation methods[61].

---

[58] Long-term use of earth batteries on a plot of land can cause an over-accumulation of copper or other forms of metal-toxicity, eventually leading to crop failure.

[59] Since it would allow for increased production for a one-time nominal amount of setup and labor costs. This is compared to the post-WWI chemical companies looking for recurring revenue streams through the continual use of synthetic fertilizers.

[60] (Black, 1971)

[61] (Chopra)

In experiments run by scientists Andrew Goldsworthy, a specialist in plant biotechnology at Imperial College in London, and Keerti Singh Rathore, who received his PhD from there as well (now associate professor and director of the Laboratory for Crop Transformation at Texas A&M University), tiny electrodes were used to deliver minuscule amounts of electrical current for long periods to the cells of tobacco plants, using a technique known as tissue culture. The results turned out to be extraordinary, revealing plant growth rates approximately 70 percent greater than average. The plants also put out up to five times as many shoots.

These same results were also found to be true for experiments on callus cultures. Callus is basically undifferentiated tissue that grows over the surface of the wound on an injured plant to protect it. Callus cultures were created by placing a few small pieces of plant onto an agar gel containing sugar, mineral salts, and a selection of vitamins and hormones to simulate what a plant would normally receive as nourishment from the rest of the plant. When microamps of current were passed through the cells, their growth was accelerated. Other potential explanations were negated by the fact that the same results occurred when the polarity of the currents were reversed[62].

A couple of studies from the Philippines found what they called "electrogenic" stimulation to have resulted in "a significant influence on plant height at maturity, number of pods per plant and, length and weight of pods per plant," demonstrating electricity's effectiveness on both growth characteristics and yield[63].

A University of Maryland study, mentioned in a 1984 edition of *Mother Earth News*, showed that a sizable increase in plant growth could be obtained by applying an electric field to plant roots. One of the tests involved 26 *salvia* plants. Of these, 14 were electrified using the current from a solar cell, while the remaining 12 in the control group were grown normally. After four weeks, the average

---

[62](Goldsworthy, 1986)
[63](Arcinue, 1982)

Chapter 3: The History of Growing with Electricity 37

height of the electrified group was 10.5 inches while the average of the control group was only 5.5 inches[64].

Lastly, it's worth mentioning that experimenters from within the Electric Fertilizer community have been sharing their own results... Ranging from Russ who is currently working on replicating some experiments he ran in the 80s, using high-voltage electric fields to stimulate corn growth, to Weber & Lang, a father & son team who are obsessed with electroculture and its effect on tomatoes.

Results of One of Weber & Lang's Experimental Trials

For instance, in one of their trials (results shown above), they obtained an increase in yield of approximately 40 percent by weight (left image). The following growing season, they achieved gains of 50 percent by weight while also increasing the speed of growth such that they were able to harvest fruit almost a month earlier than the control group plants.

---
[64](Byers, 1984)

Summary

For a long time people have had great success experimenting with the application of electricity to plants. Using direct current (DC), a form of electricity that's easy to generate, a whole range of beneficial results has been produced. Seed and soil fertility has been increased. Yields and fruit size have been increased. Even fungal infections have been thwarted. The implications of this research are quite vast. From the individual looking to grow his own food in a very limited space to whole communities that cannot supply enough food, this technology can be used to quadruple yields, increasing not only the size of foodstuffs, but nutrient content and flavor as well. Furthermore, these results can be obtained without the use of synthetic chemical fertilizers or GMO-based seeds.

In the next section, we'll start looking into the fundamentals of the background processes that are involved. By getting a primer on these mechanisms, you will have a better understanding of what's going on in your own garden. This knowledge will help you go beyond the information contained in this book so you can improve the process yourself.

Chapter 4: The Fundamentals of Soil Science

The science of soil is very complex, covering inorganic, organic and electrochemistry, biology, physics, geology, geophysics and other fields of study. The purpose of this chapter is to discuss the basics of soil science as it applies to electroculture in order to set the stage for understanding both why it brings such enormous benefits and why it isn't always successful.

The Structure of Soil

While soil may seem like a very basic material on which plants grow and through which worms and other insects burrow, it is actually a very complex and diverse set of living and non-living substances. What's amazing is how well the different soil components interact with each other, to create a beneficial environment that is suited for the development, nourishment and sustainability of all of its life forms.

The structure of soil is varied and complex. It is made of air, water, mineral particles, organic matter and organisms, too. In between the soil particles are empty areas called pore spaces, which are typically half air and half water. While soil is mostly composed of mineral particles, depending on the fertility of the soil, organic matter may also be present. It's the organic materials present in soil that are essential in holding soil particles together, storing nutrients and feeding soil organisms.

Chapter 4: The Fundamentals of Soil Science   40

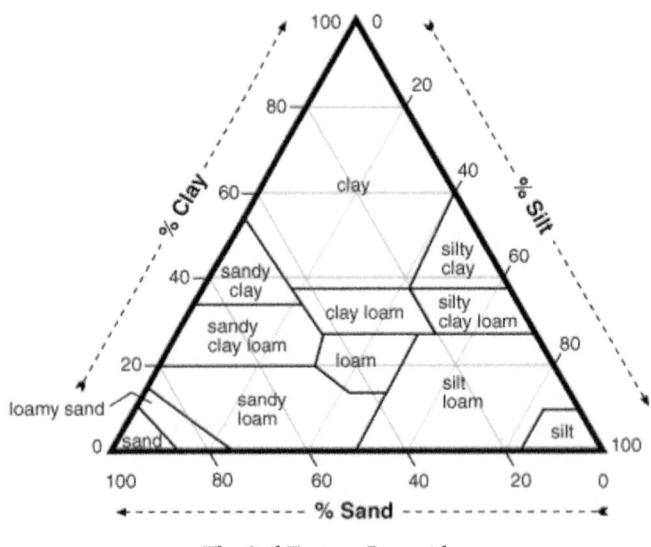

The Soil Texture Pyramid

Source: Natural Resources Conservation Service

Soils are categorized into three groups: clay, silt and sand. Soil texture depends on the proportion of particles from each of these groups. For example, loam has similar proportions of all three classes of particles. While a sandy loam is higher in sand, a clay loam is higher in clay.

The University of Minnesota Agricultural Extension offers the following details on soil structure:

"Soil particles rarely exist by themselves. Typically they will naturally come together into tiny clumps called micro-aggregates that eventually bind together with others to form larger aggregates. In ideal soil conditions, the structure will consist of a wide range of aggregate and pore sizes."

Soil Types & Properties

As described above, a wide array of soil combinations are possible by mixing different types of soil together into various forms of aggregates. Below are some basic characteristics of the different soil types:

Property	Sand	Loam	Clay
Nutrient storage	Poor	Good	Excellent
Water infiltration	Excellent - Unless it's water repelling or compacted	Good - Unless compacted	Poor - Water that tends to pool/not drain tends to suffocate some plant roots.
Water holding capacity	Poor - Requires frequent watering	Good	Excellent
Aeration	Good - Unless compacted	Good - Unless compacted	Poor

Soil Types & Properties

Aggregate Formation

Microbes decomposing organic matter create compounds that glue soil particles together. Like getting sticky fingers from eating cotton candy, sugars that are excreted from plant roots cause clumping. Humus, which refers to stable organic matter that has been fully broken down, also binds soil particles together. Fungal hyphae, collectively called mycelium also have a role in stabilizing aggregates. Soils are further enhanced through the activities of insects, earthworms and other larger organisms when they burrow through the soil. These organisms also deposit fecal matter which becomes stable soil aggregates, over time. When plants and animals decompose on the surface, the resulting residue and organic matter improves soil structure by becoming food for fungi and bacteria that in turn help keep the process going indefinitely.

In addition to the biological activities that support the formation of soil structure, physical and chemical processes present are also important. Physical actions such as freezing and thawing cycles affect soil structure just as much as wetting and drying, compaction by animals or machinery, or the movement of roots pushing and extending themselves through the soil. Chemically, electrostatic charges help to bind minerals to larger particles together, creating different forms of minerals, clays and so on.

Next, remember that the ground is not simply made up of a uniform field of soil particles. In real life it is composed of a great range of textures that vary depending upon geographical region, how the land has been treated, and based on the presence of other forms of life (e.g. bacteria, worms, moles, and others). Take for example rocky soils from a mountainous region. In this case you can expect the topsoil to be filled with a mix of clays, sands, gravels, organic matter and a certain amount of larger rocks or boulders. Other variations in land may include a change in the way minerals or the soil type is laid out in any given area.

When planting your crop, it's important that seeds be sown on loose soil composed of living, fertile topsoil. Loose soils give plant roots plenty of room to push through the soil, accessing water and nutrients with ease. When soils become hard and compacted, not only is it more difficult for the roots to grow outward and locate new nutrient sources, but root access to water can become too restricted.

Chapter 4: The Fundamentals of Soil Science   43

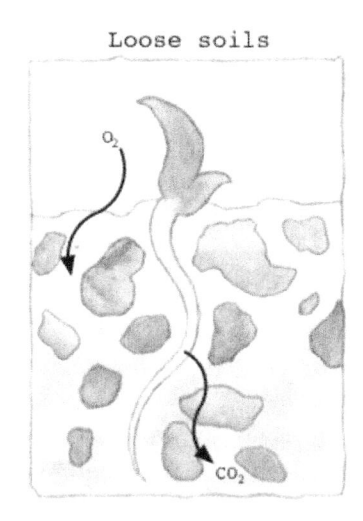

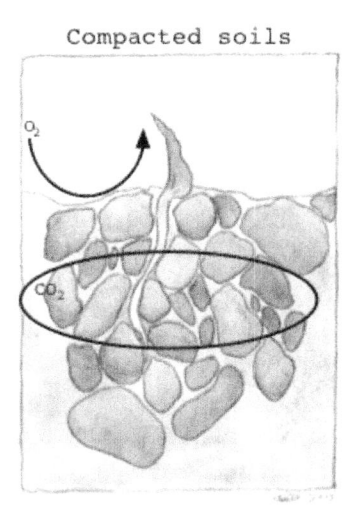

Differences Between Loose and Compacted Soils

Source: Based on illustration from ClayDoctor.com[65]

Understanding the type of soil you're growing on is essential for designing an electroculture system. For instance, one of the effects of electrical soil stimulation is the induced movement of water and/or nutrients through the soil. Soils with high clay content have a much greater ionic mobility, which in turn means plants can grow better, not only due to the intrinsic nutrient availability, but even more so due to the increasing nutrient mobility from electrical stimulation. Sandy soils, by contrast, do not have as much mobility of nutrients to start with, so the impact from electrical stimulation will be not be as great.

The Nutrient Cycle

Soil, as the storehouse for nutrients that plants need to consume for growth, is a diverse and dynamic environment where soil

---

[65] http://www.claydoctor.com/

organisms, nutrients, water, and other forms of matter essential for life are continually in action. Roots draw in dissolved minerals and water that are found withing pores spaces. Since the amount of nutrients present in the soil solution at any one time is just a fraction of that needed by plants over the course of the year, the water-soluble nutrient mix must be continually replenished with minerals and organic matter. Over time, especially with monocropping and the use of toxic pest and weed control agents, the availability of soil nutrients diminishes over time. To get around this, many growers manually amend their soils by adding in readily available fertilizers once or more each year. A growing trend is the movement towards the use of organic nutrients (compared to the addition of just nitrogen, phosphorous or potassium) in various forms ranging from well-conditioned mulches and composts, to cover crops as well. Generally speaking, soil particles and plant residues are made of large quantities of nutrients that are nutritionally-unavailable, so other means of transformation (e.g. bacteria and fungi) are needed to break them down into forms that plants can take in and use. Over time, plant residues eventually decompose into soil particulates, mineral ions, or reform into humus.

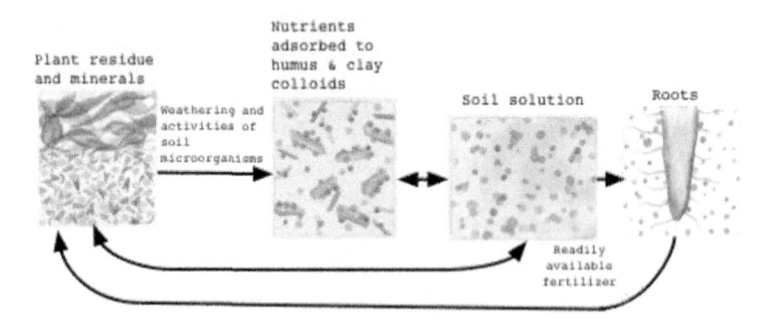

Forms of Plant Nutrients

Source: Based on University of Minnesota Extension[66]

While clay and humus are not absorbed by plants, they hold

---

[66]http://www.extension.umn.edu/distribution/cropsystems/components/7399_02.html

nutrients in the form of mineral ions on their surfaces. The number of places that are available to hold nutrients is called the exchange capacity, or more specifically, the Cation Exchange Capacity (CEC) of the soil. Cations, or positively charged ionic elements, are held together by electrostatic forces. Cationic elements include:

Alkaline Cations	Acidic Cations
Calcium (Ca^{2+})	Hydrogen (H^{1+})
Magnesium (Mg^{2+})	Aluminum (Al^{3+})
Potassium (K^{1+})	
Sodium (Na^{1+})	

Common Soil Cations

How are these used? Since cations are electrostatically bonded to soil particles, they are easily exchangeable with others cations and are therefore readily available for plant uptake. Through a process in the root hairs, ionic nutrients are released into the soil solution where they then become available for use.

Because clay soils tend to have more organic matter present than sandy soils, the CEC value of clay tends to be higher than that of sand. Increasing the organic matter content of any soil will help to increase the CEC because it also holds cations like the clays. However, as topsoil disappears due to erosion and other factors, our soils have smaller amounts of organic matter. As a result, modern topsoils have fewer nutrients available than topsoils containing rich amounts of humus[67].

As plants draw nutrients out of the soil solution, more may be released into the solution from exchange sites present on clay and humus particles. When chemical fertilizers are added to soil, they aren't necessarily directly used by plants. Instead, like minerals from other sources, they become attached to exchange sites. Once they are situated within the soil mass, they are then consumed by microorganisms which transform them into forms that can be

---
[67](Lippert)

absorbed by plant roots[68].

Once the nutrients are released from the soil and absorbed by the root hairs, they are moved inside the plant. Note that the cells and extracellular fluid within the roots themselves have a higher concentration of nutrients used to sustain the plant's life compared to the concentration present in the soil. To get around this "concentration gradient" that would normally prevent soil-based nutrients from getting inside of the roots, a number of electrochemical and biophysical processes (e.g. ion pumps) are used to bring these substances in. Once inside, they are transported throughout the plant. These processes will be covered in more detail later on.

Since nutrients are typically bound to soil particles, plant roots extract nutrients through three main mechanisms:

- The root grows into an area where the soil solution has not been depleted of nutrients and starts absorbing nutrients from the soil particles via fine root hairs.
- When a root depletes the nutrients near it, additional nutrients often diffuse into the deficient area, depending upon the moisture level and the nature of the soil.
- Or, through mass flow, like after a rain shower, water flows towards the root and carries nutrients towards it.

In summary, the fertility of soil is affected by a number of factors:

- Amount of nutrients in the soil	- Soil mix with adequate water infiltration and holding capacity
- Nutrient availability	- Recurring source of organic matter
- Good rooting environment	- Active beneficial soil bacteria
- Uncompacted soil structure	- Proper temperature level
- Adequate water	- Appropriate pH

Factors Affecting Soil Fertility

---
[68](Lippert)

Soil Bacteria

Bacteria are tiny one-celled organisms that are found everywhere. In soil, a teaspoon of productive soil generally contains between 100 million and 1 billion bacterial organisms. They typically fall within one of the following functional groups:

- Decomposers
- Mutualists
- Pathogens
- Lithotrophs

The most common type of soil bacteria is the decomposer that consumes simple carbon compounds, such as root fluids and fresh plant litter. Bacteria-based decomposing processes convert energy from organic matter into forms useful to the rest of the soil food web. Decomposers are especially important in immobilizing or retaining nutrients in their cells, thus preventing a loss of nutrients. For example, decomposition keeps nitrogen in a water-soluble form in the rooting zone rather than its normal gaseous form, which can easily escape into the atmosphere. Mutualists form partnerships with plants - the most well-known of them are nitrogen-fixing bacteria.

Bacterial pathogens can be harmful to plants. They include kinds like *Erwinia*, and certain species of *Agrobacterium*. Lithotrophs or chemoautotrophs obtain their energy from compounds of nitrogen, sulfur, iron, or hydrogen instead of carbon compounds. On the other hand, some of these species are important to nitrogen cycling and the degradation of pollutants.

One of the most well-known beneficial types of bacteria are nitrogen-fixing bacteria called *Rhizobia* which are normally present in soils where legumes grow. Nitrogen from the air is "fixed" or brought into the plant via a process where the bacteria infects the root hairs of plants. Once infected, a symbiotic relationship ensues where the bacteria is fed from exudates or chemicals that are released from the roots, and in return, the plant receives a consumable form of nitrogen that is needed for growth.

All these organisms, from tiny bacteria up to the large earthworms and insects, interact with one another in a multitude of ways within the soil ecosystem. Organisms not directly involved in decomposing plant wastes may feed on each other, each others' waste products, or other released substances. Among the materials released by the various microbes are vitamins, amino acids, sugars, antibiotics, gums and waxes. Bacteria and other soil organisms perform important services related to water dynamics, nutrient cycling and disease suppression.

Summary

In this chapter we covered the basics of soil science: what soils are made of, how they are made, some characteristics of different types of soils and a brief overview of the types of organisms that live in the soil, who assist with the formation of soil structure and benefiting plant growth.

In the next chapter we'll dive into the invisible world of electricity and the charges present within the soil. The role of electrical charge, ions, chemicals and more will help with building your understanding of electrochemical processes in soil, which is critical for getting a solid understanding of the science behind electroculture.

Chapter 5: Electrical Properties of Soils

In this chapter we're going to jump into the science of soils from an electrical perspective. What this means is that we're primarily going to focus on soils as an electrolytic medium, or in other words, its ability to conduct electricity.

Due to the results of the soil-forming process, the distribution and movement of electrical charges in soils can vary quite drastically, usually due to the following properties:

- The types & charges of materials
- Moisture levels
- Cation Exchange Capacity (also known as the CEC)
- And more.

Since ionic compounds present in soil tend to clump together due to their intrinsically charged nature (since positive charged particles tend to be electrically attracted to negatively charged ones), soil aggregates of varying net charge will collect in various regions of a given soil mass. The difference in charge between any two or more regions of the soil will result in a voltage difference between those regions (albeit a very small one). Any time a voltage is present within the soil, it implies that there will also be an electric field present, too.

Chemical properties such as humus content, CEC, mineral composition, and the amount of soluble salts all have an influence on how ions are exchanged within soils. Nutrient availability, pH and the degree of how easily ions are adsorbed and desorbed from soil particles determine the overall functionality of a soil with regards to its ability to support life.

Electrical Resistivity and Conductivity

Electrical resistivity is a physical property that describes how well a particular material resists the flow of electric current through it. According to Ohm's Law, Voltage(V)= Current(I) x Resistance(R). As shown in the diagram below, the amount of resistance of a particular material is based on its geometry and volume.

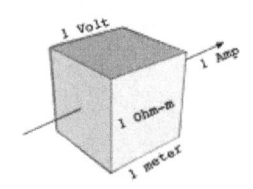

Graphical definition of voltage, current and resistivity

Thus the resistivity, ρ(rho), of a material is the resistance per unit volume, which is measured in terms of Ohm-meters, or Ohm-m (Ω-m).

In soil science, the inverse of resistivity is often used. This is known as the Conductivity, σ (sigma), and can be calculated from resistivity by simply taking its inverse, or $\sigma = 1/\rho$ which is measured in units called Siemens per meter (S/m).

The electrical conductivity of earth-based materials varies over many orders of magnitude due to many factors including: rock type, porosity, connectivity of pores, nature of the soil fluids and metallic content held within the earth's matrix of solids. A very rough indication of the range of conductivity for rocks and minerals is shown in the following figure.

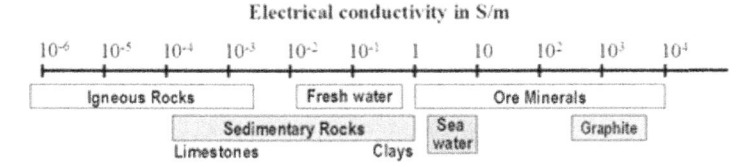

Electrical Conductivities of Different Types of Soils

Source: University of British Columbia[69]

Soil Composition and Resistivity

While basic soil types vary in terms of particle size, structure and consistency, depending upon the amount of organic matter, the conductivity of the soil will vary. Black dirt or soils with high levels of organic matter are usually good conductors because they retain high moisture levels and have more electrically conductive substances present. Because sandy soils drain quickly, they subsequently have a low moisture content. Any ionic matter found within the sand/soil solution is minimized because it is easily washed away. The net result of which is a higher electrical resistance. Solid rock and volcanic ash contain virtually no moisture or electrolytes (ionic compounds in solution) and hence have very high levels of resistivity.

Electrical resistivity is the most variable of all geophysical properties of rocks because of the enormous range of values that are possible, ranging as much as 10 orders of magnitude. The next chart illustrates in a general way how the resistivities of rock groups compare to each other.

[69] http://www.eos.ubc.ca/ubcgif/iag/foundations/properties/resistivity.htm

Chapter 5: Electrical Properties of Soils   52

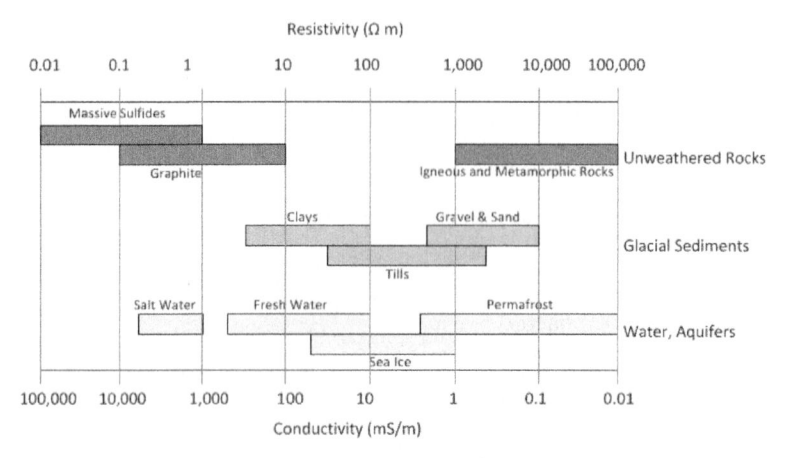

Resistivities of Various Rock Groups

Source: University of British Columbia[70]

As shown in the chart, note how each vertical bar is a 10 times increase or decrease in conductivity or resistivity. Considering that the growth of plants is affected by electrochemical soil interactions (See Chapter 6), the natural occurrence of different types of rocks and their presence in the soil may have a huge influence on soil fertility.

Composed mostly of silicate minerals, soils and rocks are essentially insulators with the following exceptions: magnetite, specular hematite, carbon, graphite, pyrite and pyrrhotite. Since most rocks are resistive in nature, the electrical conductivity of soils is primarily due to the presence of electrolytes[71] and carbon itself. As stated before, the conductivity of soil depends on a number of factors:

- Porosity
- Hydraulic permeability[72]
- Moisture content
- Concentration of dissolved electrolytes

---
[70] http://ow.ly/dokkh
[71] Electrolytes are liquids containing mobile chemical ions
[72] The term *permeability* describes how soil pores are interconnected

- Temperature and phase of pore fluid
- Amount and composition of colloids

The structure of soil and its moisture has a huge effect on soil fertility. This is due in part to the ability of soluble nutrients to flow across pore boundaries and to be available for uptake by root systems. When the soil is non-compacted and porous, the soil has a greater water capacity and thus has a greater capacity to hold onto electrolytic fluids. Non-compacted soils also have a greater capacity to store and make available gases like nitrogen and oxygen.

In contrast to the above charts which compare the relative conductivities of rocks, a similar comparison can be made on fluids, e.g. the concentration of ions in a given amount of fluid, also known as salinity. For example:

- Tap water has a minimal conductivity of around .01 S/m with a salinity of about 40 ppm (parts per million)
- Seawater has a rough conductivity of 3.3 S/m with a salinity of 30,000 ppm.

Since seawater has a greater conductance and a much greater measure of salinity compared to tap water, it conducts electricity much easier. While salts allow for greater amounts of soil conductivity, they also need to be controlled since the presence of too much salt in the soil can harm plant life. While the presence of electrolytes is needed to promote the healthy growth of plants, it needs to be balanced as either too little or too much can be harmful as well.

It has been found that plants respond favorably to growing in warmer areas. This may be due to the fact that the temperature of the ground affects ionic mobility since it increases with temperature. Higher temperatures means more nutrients are available to be desorbed from soil particles and into the soil solution.

The electrical resistivity/conductivity of soils is rather complicated, with many factors affecting it. One of the biggest contributing factors that makes the measurement of conductivity difficult is that land areas are typically non-uniform. What this means is that no matter how smooth the ground looks from above, it is really composed of a mixture of topsoil, clays, rocks and minerals, decayed matter, and likely other materials, too. Furthermore, the fact that all of these components are of different sizes create situations where the land mass contains a large range of pore sizes. Since resistivity is primarily related to porosity, it becomes difficult to know the true conductivity of soil, especially in the case of measuring it on open land. On the other hand, in controlled environments such as raised beds and potted plants, the conductivity is much more likely to be uniform.

Table of (Approximate) Soil Resistivities (Ω-cm)			
Soil Type	Average	Min	Max
Fills: ashes, cinders, brine wastes	2,370	590	7,000
Clay, shale, gumbo, loam	4,060	340	16,300
Clay etc with varying amounts of sand and gravel	15,800	1,020	135,000
Gravel, sand, stones with a little clay and loam	94,000	59,000	458,000

Table: Soil Types and Associated Electrical Resistivity

Source: PEMA[73]

As shown in the chart above, since the variation in soil resistivity is very large, it becomes difficult to make an assessment of soil resistivity based on soil type alone. It's also worth noting that most topsoils have been treated in some ways via the addition of various fertilizers or amendments. Here's a list of some common soil additives in relation to their resistivity:

---

[73]http://www.pema.ie/PDFs/App-Ground-SoilResistivity.pdf

Chapter 5: Electrical Properties of Soils

Amendment Type	Resistivity (Ohm-m)
Cow waste, mixed with sand (dry)	1354
Cow waste, mixed with sand (wet)	9.88
Chicken waste (dry)	806
Chicken waste (wet)	5.8
Ashes (wet)	1
Sawdust (wet)	112.28
Garden soil (dry)	1200
Garden soil (wet)	32

Table: Soil Amendments and Associated Electrical Resistivity

Source: Electrical properties of biological wastes used as effective soil conditioners for electrical earthing[74]

Next we move onto soil porosity. The moisture content of soil has the greatest influence on conductivity because it is the primary medium that carries current via the chemical ions present within pore-water.

Moisture content % by weight	Resistivity (Ω-cm)	
	Top Soil	Sandy Loam
0	> 10^9	> 10^9
2.5	250,000	150,000
5	165,000	43,000
10	53,000	18,500
15	19,000	10,500
20	12,000	6,300
30	6,400	4,200

Table: Soil Electrical Resistivity by Moisture Content

Source: PEMA[75]

It can also be influenced by local climate conditions, as shown in the next chart showing soil resistivity by temperature.

---
[74] http://nopr.niscair.res.in/bitstream/123456789/1330/1/JSIR%2066(10)%20(2007)%20873-879.pdf
[75] http://www.pema.ie/PDFs/App-Ground-SoilResistivity.pdf

Temperature		Resistivity
C	F	(Ω-cm)
20	68	7,200
10	50	9,900
0	32 (water)	13,800
0	32 (ice)	30,000
-5	23	79,000
-15	14	330,000

Table: Soil Electrical Resistivity by Temperature

Source: PEMA[76]

The next largest set of factors that influence resistivity are electrolytic, a topic that will be covered in greater detail in the next chapter.

Summary

Had you ever imagined that there would be a relationship between soil and its composition with regards to electricity? Who would have known that soils are naturally electric in that they hold and transport charge? The fact of the matter is that most life is electrical, for electricity allows for cellular communications, nutrient absorption, the turning on and off of proteins, ion channels, and a slew of other bioelectrical processes. It is in use everywhere, in the creation and sustaining of all kinds of life. It's only natural that soil itself would also be electric, and why not? After all, back in Chapter 2 we learned that the air was naturally electrical. In the following chapters, we will learn how applied electrical stimuli affects soil chemistry, structure and living organisms, too.

---

[76] http://www.pema.ie/PDFs/App-Ground-SoilResistivity.pdf

Chapter 6: Soil Electrochemistry

In this chapter, the topics of soil science and electrochemistry will be described with respect to how they interrelate with each other. It turns out that a number of very interesting physical phenomena occur when electric fields are applied to materials like sand or soil. In the following sections, five physical processes will be described that will help explain how the growth of plants is affected when soils are electrically stimulated.

The main topics of the following chapter are:

- The electrolysis of water
- Electrolytes in the soil
- The effects electric fields have on soil
- The effect electric fields have on pH

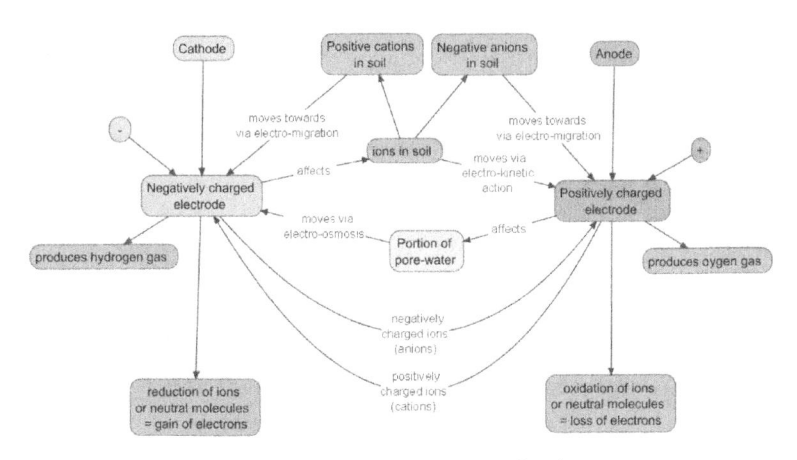

Electrochemical Mechanics of Soil

Electric Fields and Soil?

When an electric field is applied to a wet, porous medium, a number of effects can be observed: - Electrolysis
- Electro-osmosis - Electro-kinetic migration - Electro-migration - Electro-phoresis

What follows is a brief description of these terms. Later, we'll go into more detail, showing how these effects can be of benefit to your soil and crops.

Electrolysis is a term most people have heard of before. Think back to elementary or middle school when your science teacher may have demonstrated how water could be transformed into explosive hydrogen gas...this was a demonstration of electrolysis, or the splitting of water into its elemental parts.

Osmosis is another scientific term that many people have heard about, most likely in the context of water purification via reverse-osmosis. Osmosis refers to the movement of water-soluble molecules through or blocked by a semi-permeable membrane. In water purification, reverse osmosis is used to separate undesired substances out of water using a selectively porous membrane as a filter. It only allows a subset of the particles to pass while blocking other particles from passing through.

Electro-osmosis is the combination of the above. It is the electrically-driven movement of water that occurs when an electric field is applied across some amount of moist soil or sand.

The next three terms are ones that you've probably never heard of. Electro-kinetics and electro-migration are terms that basically mean the same thing. In essence, these terms refer to the movement of ions or molecules in response to an applied electric field. Electrophoresis is the movement of charged particles or colloids under electric fields. So by way of example, in the biomedical industry, a technique called gel electrophoresis is used to separate complex molecules like proteins, by charge or size. It is also used in genetics research as a way of sorting mixed populations of DNA fragments.

So the purpose of this chapter is to cover the basics of these methods, describing how each of these effects become present in soils under electrical influence.

We'll start by exploring the electrolysis reaction, followed by a brief explanation of the conductive nature of soils. From there, we'll dive into the other relevant electrochemical mechanisms mentioned above.

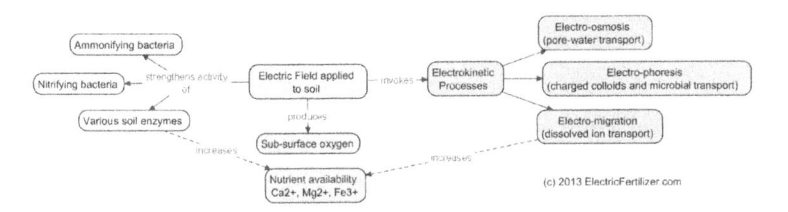

The Effect of Electricity Upon Soil Particles

The Electrolysis of Water

Back to science class... Try to recall the electrolysis experiment mentioned above. The teacher hooked up a battery to a container of water that had upside down test tubes over each electrical contact. After a short while, the teacher would say that the electricity from the battery broke down the water molecules leaving hydrogen gas in one test tube and oxygen gas in the other. The fun part of the experiment happened when they ignited both tubes and the one with the hydrogen gas would make a loud "pop!" The mechanism that allowed the water to be split into two parts is called electrolysis.

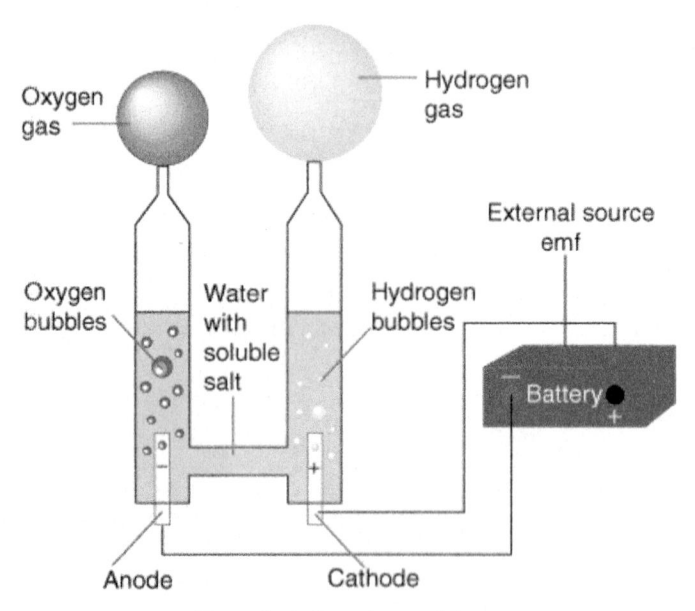

Electrolysis Experimental Setup

In an electrolysis reaction, inert or non-reactive electrodes are placed in water and a direct electrical current is passed between them. Non-reactive electrodes are typically used because if they were made of a material that reacts with any of the components of water or the electricity itself, there wouldn't be a clean split, as other compounds would be formed. Electrodes of this nature ensure that a pure split of water (H2O) molecules takes place. This causes changes to occur at the cathode or negative electrode according to Equation 1:

Equation 1: $2H_2O - 4e^- \rightarrow O_2(gas) + 4H^+$ (Known as oxidation)

At the positive(+) electrode, also known as the anode, electrons (negatively-charged) are stripped from water molecules, oxygen (O2) is released, and protons (H$^+$, or hydrogen ions) are formed which travel through the electrolyte (water) towards the negative (-) electrode, known as the cathode.

At the same time, the cathode donates electrons to water molecules creating what are called hydroxyl ions (OH-), thus liberating hydrogen gas as shown in Equation 2.

Equation 2: 4H2O + 4e- → 2H2 (gas) + 4OH- (Known as reduction)

The reason this concept is important is because it forms the basis for the application of electricity to materials containing water. Soil substances that are typically mixed with pore water include organic and inorganic chemicals and molecules, colloids, and also microorganisms.

Thus, taking these concepts and applying them to soil we end up with reactions called redox (reduction-oxidation) reactions. In the upcoming subsections, we'll cover how these reactions affect the soil.

Electrolytes in the Soil

Soils and other plant growth mediums can vary in their innate electrical conductivities ranging from being not-very-conductive like sand, to being more conductive, like clay or humus. Most soils are conductive due to the presence of dissolved chemical ions that include calcium, sodium, potassium, soluble fatty acids, nitrate, phosphate, and chloride ions. These substances, known as electrolytes, are a class of substances that contain free ions, which is what makes soils electrically conductive.

In order for soils to be conductive, they need to have a minimal amount of moisture present[77]. Most seemingly dry soils have more than 5 percent moisture which is sufficient enough to provide a continuous path for these ions to move. This is essential for plants as the roots need access to these nutrients and ion transport across cellular membranes is the means by which they extract them from soil (this will be covered later in Chapter 9). As mentioned before, the most significant feature of natural soils, especially clays, is the

---

[77]Note: The minimal moisture level needed for electrokinetic transport to be effective is approximately 25 percent of saturation. (Lindgren, 1994)](#Lindgren-1994)

high Cation Exchange Capacity (CEC) which provides plants with greater access to the nutrients that are available.

Application of Electric Fields to Soil

As previously explained, osmosis occurs when water along with other particular substances, are allowed to pass through a semi-permeable membrane. On the other hand, electro-osmosis(EO) describes a totally different effect. When an externally applied electrical field is applied to a porous medium such as soil, the pore-water begins to flow from the area around the positive electrode towards that of the negative electrode! So, when a direct current(DC)-based electric field is applied to an area of soil, it moves a portion of the pore water toward the cathode(-)[78]. This can be visualized by looking at the image on the left in the following illustration.

In a similar manner, through a process called electro-migration(EM), negative ions in the soil will be electrically driven toward the positive electrode(anode), while at the same time, positively charged substances are driven toward the negative electrode(cathode)[79]. It's effectively the transport of chemical ions without the help of electro-osmotic fluid flow. This can be visualized by looking at the image in the center in the next illustration.

So how fast do these ions move? Well, the speed at which these substances move under the soil is on the order of 5-20cm/day[80] in fine sands and smaller grain structures like kaolinite clay. The speed also depends on the polarity and strength of ionic charge. Since strong cations have a strong positive charge, they have a tendency to be adsorbed to soil particles because of the soil's innate negative charge. Weaker cations will be weakly attracted to soil particles, making them more mobile. Since anions have a negative charge and tend to move away (via electrostatic repulsion) from the soil

---

[78](Ferrarese, 2008) p.21, (Alshawabkeh,2001)
[79](Ferrarese, 2008) p.25, (Alshawabkeh,2001)
[80]Via US Patent #6,086,739

Chapter 6: Soil Electrochemistry   63

particles, they will flow through the soil mass much more easily than cations[81].

Moving up in the scale of particles that can be electrically-moved is the process of electro-phoresis(EP) which is a similar mechanism where charged particles, colloids or even cells or microbes can be moved by electric fields[82]. As mentioned above, electrophoretic transport can include proteins and other biological substances including microbial species like bacteria. This can be visualized by looking at the image on the right in the following illustration.

So it is in the following ways that a number of effects can occur that may or may not be of benefit to your land, including:

- The electro-migratory transport of macro- and micro-nutrients away from soil particles where they are held, to accumulation in pore-water.
- The transport of root exudates in a similar manner.
- The spreading of soil amendments.

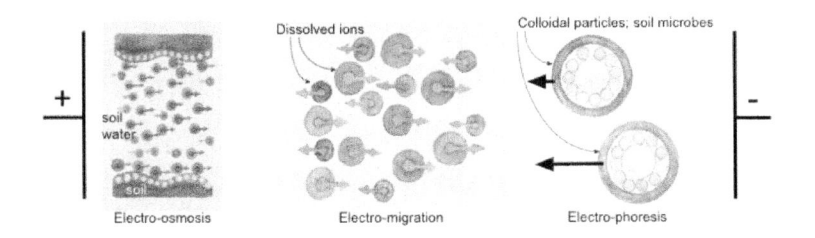

Electrokinetic Processes in a DC Field

Source: Bill Perry based on Wieczorek

While much is known about modern soil science, much more research is needed to show the effect of these applied fields to soil. More study is needed to determine the effects that occur under a

---
[81](Lindgren, 1994)
[82](Ferrarese, 2008) p.26, (Alshawabkeh,2001)

Chapter 6: Soil Electrochemistry 64

wide range of soil conditions with respect to the wide variety of ores, minerals, and other complex or crystalline compounds found in soils.

> The advantage of using electricity for nutrient transport underground is that it can be very effective in spreading nutrients throughout a region comprised of varied land and soil conditions. Over 100 years ago, it was written that electroculture has been found to be a very effective method for inexpensively spreading fertilizer throughout a field[83].

Looking at the soil pyramid and seeing that soils vary primarily between sand and clay, it makes sense that the performance of electro-osmosis, electro-kinesis, and electro-phoresis will differ under the wide variety of soil conditions that are possible. Furthermore, since the structure and components of most ground-based soils (compared to container-based soils) are predominantly non-uniform, especially as the area of ground increases in size, the electrochemical effects of these phenomena are not completely known in large scale growing environments, and thus their behavior can only be estimated.

Effect on pH

pH Basics

With all of the electrically-induced ionic and water-based transport occurring within the soil, one side effect that can have a significant impact is the change to soil pH. For those who don't know, soil pH is a measure of the acidity or basicity of soils which affects how available nutrients are for uptake by the plants. It is expressed as a

---
[83](McLeod, 1892)

Chapter 6: Soil Electrochemistry   65

negative logarithm of the hydrogen concentration on a scale from 1.0 to 14.0. Values below 7.0 are considered acidic while those above 7.0 are considered basic or alkaline. A pH of 7.0 is defined as neutral.

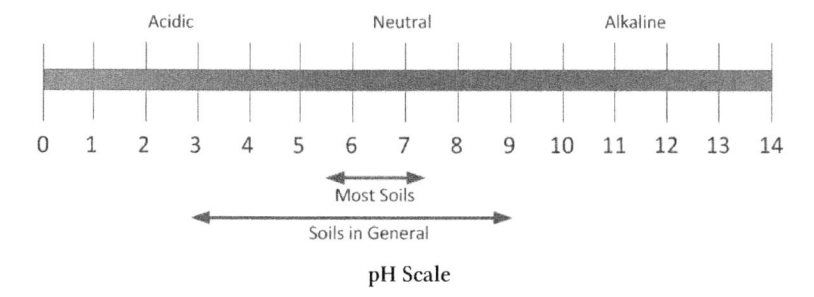

pH Scale

In terms of the preferences of plants, note that most plants prefer (slightly) acidic to neutral soils, so let's begin by noting how soils become acidic in the first place. While you may know that pH is a measure of the number of hydrogen ions in a solution, when it comes to soils, the amount released into the soil is also a function of the number of aluminum (Al^{3+}) ions also present in the soil solution. Aluminum has an interesting property in that it reacts with water in such a way that causes a 3x release in the number of H+ ions, causing rapid acidification of soils. Other processes that can make soils more acidic include:

- Fertilizer usage
- Plant root activity
- Weathering of minerals
- Acid rain

pH in Electroculture

Referring to electrolysis reactions shown in Equations 1 and 2, when electric current is passed through a solution, the hydrolysis, or separation of water, is initiated. This results in either oxidation or reduction half-reactions that occur in the electrodes, which results in a change in pH.

However, in soil, full reduction-oxidation reactions (also known as redox reactions) take place resulting in a neutral or near-neutral pH level once the full set of reactions take place. This explains why most of the soil under the electric field will maintain an overall neutral pH, except for those portions of soil very close to the electrodes where there may be a predominant amount of hydrogen or hydroxyl ions. This abundance in H^+ or OH^- will result in an increase in the soil's acidity or alkalinity levels, respectively.

Since soil becomes acidic at the anode (+) and alkaline at the cathode (-), the H^+ ions (protons) generated at the anode eventually begin to propagate towards the cathode. They move electro-kinetically towards the cathode because opposite charges attract. This traveling set of hydrogen ions, is known as an acidic or "acid" front. It serves to further aid in releasing ions that that have been adhered to soil particles, increasing the mobilizing effect. The result is that it thus helps nutrients that are bound to soil particles to become loose and more available for uptake by neighboring plants. Conversely, the mobilized OH^- ions via reduction are collectively called an alkaline or "basic" front. The acid front moves faster than the basic front because of the higher mobility of the H^+ ions compared to the OH^- ions. Furthermore, since the direction of electro-osmotic flow is toward the negative electrode, it helps promote its propagation, too.

Up to a point, certain benefits are derived as a result from an increase in soil acidification. As the acid front moves toward the negative terminal, it can cause dissolution of minerals and other more complex nutrients. Yet, if the electric field is present for a long time, the soil will become more acidic throughout its volume except very near the cathodic(-) zone where hydroxyl ions are in abundance.

As the soil becomes more acidic, it can also bring about beneficial

Chapter 6: Soil Electrochemistry   67

effects for the cellular mechanisms within the plant. Bacteria species are tolerant to a pH between 5.0 and 9.0[84]. The most benefit to plants comes from soils in a pH range of 6.0 to 6.5, which can include:

- Major increases in nutrient availability, uptake and assimilation
- Increases in leaf respiration
- Increases in root respiration which helps nitrogen fixing bacteria
- Increases in nitrogen-fixing bacterial action leads to increases in nutrient uptake, increased growth rate and cell elongation.

On the flip-side, if the soil becomes too acidic, the performance and health of plants will begin to suffer. At a pH of 5.0 to 4.0, a number of side effects may begin to occur such as the slowing down of the activity of bacterial decomposers. Nutrients would then be tied up in their higher forms, unavailable for uptake. When the soil becomes acidic to a more extreme level, e.g. below 4.0, it then becomes possible that certain elements may become too available, leading to hydrogen, aluminum, or iron toxicity. These can directly damage root cell membranes and cause other adverse effects.

> The Risks of Aluminum Toxicity
>
> "Al [aluminum] damages roots in several ways: In root tips Al interferes with the uptake of Ca [calcium], an essential nutrient, as well as binds with phosphate and interferes with production of ATP and DNA, both of which contain phosphate. Al can also restrict cell wall expansion causing roots to become stunted." via Wikipedia[85]

---
[84](Alshawabkeh, 2001)
[85]http://en.wikipedia.org/wiki/Soil_pH

Chapter 6: Soil Electrochemistry   68

To see the relationship between soil pH and nutrient availability, the following chart shows how nutrients like nitrogen become less available as the pH drops below 6.0 and others like trace elements drop off above 6.0. Thus, keeping the pH in balance while applying electroculture becomes increasingly important, especially over longer periods of time due to the travelling acid and base fronts.

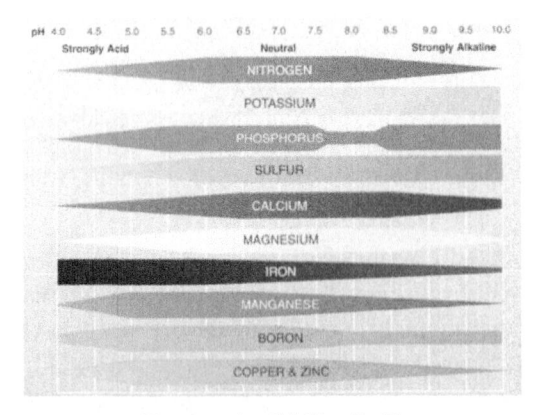

Nutrient Availability & pH

Source: Extension.org[86]

It is worth noting that if deleterious long-term electrification effects are observed due to pH problems, the growing area can be remedied through augmentation of the soil with buffering compounds such as lime. Amendments can replace the over-abundance of free hydrogen ions while also supplying additional nutrients to the soil like calcium and magnesium. Liming also helps with making macro-nutrients like phosphorus more available. Alternatively or in-conjunction with liming, the reversal of the electric-field polarity can be helpful as well by causing a reversal of the acid/base fronts.

---
[86]http://www.extension.org/pages/13064/soil-ph-modification#.VAX8fPldXXp

So what happens when the acid front eventually comes in contact with the basic front? When the two fronts collide within the soil mass, water is formed and a sharp change in pH is experienced. This can also be harmful to plants. For this reason, it is advised to running the system for too long in a continuous manner. Of course, this depends on a number of variables including the amount of voltage applied to the system as well as the distance between the electrodes, too.

Plants that grow in different soil conditions with different pH ranges often cannot grow under any different soil conditions. Considering that the movement of pH through each number on the scale results in a logarithmic increase of 10x, (e.g. A pH rise of 7.0 to 8.0 is a 10x increase; 5.0 to 7.0 is a 100x increase, and so on), many plants cannot thrive in soils that are outside of their normal pH ranges. It is for this reason that pH is covered here. So for the most part, especially while operating at low voltages over long distances, the rate of pH movement will be so small that it will likely not pose any problems.

Summary

Through the various physical processes that take place within soils as a direct response to the application of electric fields, we can now appreciate a basic understanding of the possible reasons behind the increase in growth. Covered later will be other ideas. One of which could be the release of large amounts of soil nutrients due to electrokinetic effects. We can also see that the acidification of the soils can also be a factor. Lastly, due to the release of oxygen from the electrolysis reaction, an increase in sub-soil oxygen levels can also be expected[87]. In the coming chapters we'll go deeper into these and other factors that contribute to the gains that can be realized

---

[87] This is due according to "microconductor" principle, redox reactions also occur simultaneously at all soil-pore water interfaces. (Ferrarese, 2008, p.57)

through the application of electric fields to soils.

Chapter 7: Benefits of Electroculture On Soil

Let's begin looking at the effects of electric fields on soils. Improvement of soil fertility is the primary benefit. It does this by improving the actual structure of the soil, making it light and porous which improves the growth of plants by creating areas for more water infiltration and places for roots to easily access more nutrients. Also, through both electrochemical reactions and enhanced microbial activities, the breakdown of complex nutrients can occur, making plant nutrient uptake much more available.

Soil Structure

The application of electricity to soil creates a number of effects on the actual structure of soil. It increases the granular structure and decreases the bulk density of soil by chemically increasing the size of soil aggregates, while also increasing humification. This has the end result of greatly increasing the soil's moisture retaining capacity.

The increase in humification occurs because of the reaction of free calcium ions with any humic acid present in the soil, which operates as follows: *"Under the effect of Ca^{2+}, calcium humate can make organic and inorganic colloids be glued together, which provides a good condition for the formation of aggregates."*[88]

This is further enhanced by naturally occurring bacteria present in the soil. Actively reproducing and metabolically-accelerated

---
[88](Wang, Ji-hong and Ya-qin)

bacteria populations work in conjunction with the plants to help fix carbon molecules that are sequestered from CO_2 in the atmosphere. The combination of additional amounts of carbon, plus the way that the microbes process the soil creates lots of nooks and crannies throughout the soil mass, thus helping with the formation of looser or more aerated soil conditions[89].

Water Capacity

The wilting point is the point in which a plant begins to use water from its own tissues for transpiration because soil-water has been exhausted. While clay soils have the capability of holding large amounts of water, the plants grown there are more likely to wilt because the soil-water tends to be tightly retained within the structure of the clay. So when growing on clay soils, it's usually difficult to improve water availability. Electroculture is a way that this restriction can be reversed, through the mechanism of electro-osmosis. Water would be electrically pulled out of clay and into the surrounding pore spaces, making growing in clay into a benefit, now that the value they provide realizable.

Another way the wilting point can be lowered is through the research of Wang, et. al., mentioned above. He demonstrated that applied electric fields increase the pore volume of the soil (via bacterial interactions), thus giving the soil itself an increase in water-holding capacity. This is similar to the way that a sponge with large holes can hold much more water than a weak sponge with a bunch of smaller-sized holes.

---

[89](Weatherbee, Doug)

Oxygen Content

While the leaves of the plant require carbon dioxide for photosynthesis, the roots need oxygen for cellular respiration. Normally, plants absorb oxygen from the gases present in the pore spaces within the soil. Two ways that electroculture facilitates root oxygenation are:

1. The creation of larger soil aggregates.
2. The electrolytic generation of sub-surface oxygen.

As covered above, the soil structure can be improved through the creation of larger soil aggregates. This allows for a greater amount of air to be stored beneath the soil's surface due to the larger pore space that is available. Adding in the plant's increased rate of transpiration, it makes sense that any oxygen present in the soil will be increased improving root-based oxygenation.

The way this works is as follows: as water is taken in and used by the plant, water from the surrounding pores in the soil is sucked into the plant like a siphon. As the water gets consumed, the amount of air present below the surface will increase since it gets sucked into the now-empty pore-spaces, thus helping to oxygenate the plants' roots. Again, the usefulness of larger pore spaces for oxygenation can be seen by taking a look at the figure of compacted vs uncompacted soils in chapter 4.

Furthermore, when electrolysis reactions take place in the soil, it causes the creation of gases at soil-particle boundaries, resulting in the generation of hydrogen and oxygen gases. The production of oxygen adds to the amount of air present in the soil. This may explain Sir H. Davy's results where the seeds placed in his earth battery germinated faster at the positive pole compared to the negative pole. In electroculture, multiple effects may affect the growth of plants, where in this case it was either (or both) the metabolic acceleration or the super-oxygenation that caused the superior growth.

Experiment

This can be shown in a simple experiment you can do at home where two pieces of metal are inserted into a glass of water while connected to a battery. Over time you will see small bubbles adhering to the positive terminal in the water. This is very similar to the experiment mentioned earlier. Using lower voltages has the same effect, but generates the gases at a much slower rate compared to the use of a car-battery or other high-power voltage source.

The end result of the additional pore space and the active generation of oxygen has been found to greatly accelerate and improve the growth of plants. Methods focusing on the super-oxygenation of roots are the primary focus of growing methods like aeroculture, which have been found to have shorter grow times as well as larger and healthier forms of growth. Additionally, the oxygenation of soils helps with keeping beneficial aerobic bacterial populations in check over anaerobic bacteria which can cause harm to plants and beneficial forms of soil biota.

Nutrient Availability

In the soil, nutrients in the form of complex molecules or ionic-form chemicals (e.g. fertilizer components like NH_4, K^+, Ca^{2+} and Mg^{2+}) adhere to soil particles. Clays and humus hold these compounds exceptionally well because they hold a negative charge. Under normal conditions roots and root hairs reach-out to come in contact with soil particles or soil solution. To increase the amount of nutrient particles that they can consume, they continually grow more roots and root hairs that extend farther and farther into the soil.

When external electric fields are added to the mix, additional channels are turned on that enable greater amounts of nutrient to be available to a plant's root system.

So, electroculture takes the concept of improving nutrient availability to the next level... While later on you'll learn how plants gain an improved ability to uptake soil nutrients, the concept implied here is that plants grown under electroculture absorb nutrients from more than just the soil particles or pore-water that's local to the plant itself. In fact, under an electric field, many more available nutrients in all directions (depending upon the nutrient's electrical polarity and the electrode configuration), will be made available to the plant roots, much like a large vacuum cleaner would act - pulling in nutrients from as far as the extent of the electrodes allow.

This environment of enhanced mobility enables the nutrient uptake process to operate with greater efficiency. Furthermore, this knowledge can possibly be taken advantage of to deliberately transport desired nutrient mixes from one portion of a growing area to another.

Separation of Nutrients from Soil Particles

Where formerly plant roots needed to actively reach out to touch soil particles or into new pockets of soil solution, in the case of electroculture, the nutrients become much more available because nutrients can be removed and transported with greater ease through the soil.

Through the processes of electromigration, electrophoresis and electro-osmosis, nutrients from portions of the soil mass that are not immediately adjacent to the plant roots can be separated from the soil particles to which they are normally bound and actively transported throughout the rhizosphere[90] to become available for intake.

For instance, when naturally occurring charged nutrients are exposed to an electric field, they can be easily dissociated or knocked off of the soil particles on which they hold themselves. Once this happens, they are carried through the soil in the direction of their oppositely charged field. E.g. positively-charged nutrients like calcium (Ca^{2+}) will move in the direction of the negatively-charged pole while negatively-charged substances will be moved toward the positive pole.

Enhances Nutrient Breakdown

Scientists of the past correctly posited that the application of electric fields onto soil media causes an effect upon the chemical composition of soil. There was also a basic understanding of the how electric fields cause the electrolysis of water. Similarly to

---
[90](Niroumand, 2012)

the concept of electrolysis, there were also speculations that the presence of electricity may cause the breakup of more complex compounds into simpler ones which are more readily absorbed.

Today, it is known within the field of geochemistry, especially in the area of bioremediation, that between the amount of energy that's added to the soil nutrient solution and the amount of energy that's innately present can cause electrochemical reactions to occur. Since soils contain a very complex mix of free-floating elemental ions and molecules, the number and types of reactions that are possible are mind-blowing. In keeping with the goal of simplicity, a brief, high-level description follows.

Electric fields applied to soils and sediments can affect many soil-based compounds, causing them to be possibly mobilized, mineralized[91], or broken down by way of redox reactions that occur at all soil interfaces. One of the factors that affects the rate of geochemical reactions is the grain size of the soil. Faster and larger-scale reactions tend to occur more within clays and silts, and slower, smaller-scale reactions will occur within sands and gravels. The other major factor that affects the rate of reaction is the soil's pH, where lower pH values tend to facilitate faster reactions, thus leading to a faster breakdown of nutrients[92].

It is worth noting here that, even though the material will be repeated in the next chapter covering the effects upon bacteria, many species of bacteria exhibit increased metabolic and reproductive activities. Thus, since bacteria are known for processing simpler forms of nutrients, their increased activity will further assist with the breakdown of complex soil nutrients.

---

[91]Modification to the structures or properties of chemical structures found within soil. See (Wang, Song, Kang, 2011) for more information.
[92]Alshawabkeh, p9

> **Application Note: Increasing nutrient availability in colder-climate soils**

The use of electro-horticulture can also be beneficial in low-temperature growing regions for similar reasons. Plants that are grown in low-temperature environments may not grow as well as those in warmer locales. It is surmised that the main reason for this is a decrease in ionic transport within both the soil as well as the plant itself. In contrast to higher temperatures, where the ionic mobility tends to be higher, when the temperature drops, the flow of chemical ions is hampered.

You may have observed this while trying to operate a consumer electronic device, like a mp3 player, that's been sitting in the cold, overnight. The LCD screen is very slow to operate, and the electronics may not even turn on. When the device is moved to a warmer location, the ions within the battery return to their normal state of mobility, allowing for the easy flow of ions and the normal operation of the electronic product.

In soils, reduced ionic motion affects nutrient diffusion rates which makes normal fertilization methods less efficient. Similarly, in plants, reduced chemical movement results in slower signal transport, making plants respond and ultimately grow at a slower pace.

With electroculture, through the stimulation effects that are produced, faster ionic transport in both soil and plant can be expected, resulting in normal to accelerated growth rates, even in cold weather. Of course, since the effects of stimulation can be plant-specific, and even specific to the particular history of a given plant, this isn't guaranteed, but it is something that should be subject to more experimental testing.

Summary

In conclusion, it can be seen that the use of externally-applied electric fields in conjunction with traditional forms of fertilizer (either chemical or organic) can significantly reduce the amount of fertilizer needed due to increased diffusion, breakdown and uptake efficiencies. This can result in a significant reduction in the production cost of agricultural products, since fertilizer use can be drastically reduced, and if engineered correctly, perhaps altogether removed. A side benefit would be the simultaneous improvement of soil conditions though enhanced microbial activities.

Chapter 8: Electroculture And Soil Bacteria

Though we have already described several benefits of applying electricity to soils and plants, many more benefits can be realized. For example, the application of electricity to bacterial populations naturally present in soils can drastically improve the rate that they transform nutrients which are normally unavailable to plants into more usable forms. This chapter will cover the effects of electricity on microbes, and the potential benefits of doing so.

It is well known that the various forms of bacteria living in soil provides a number of benefits for plants and soils alike. One form of bacteria called *Rhizobium* lives in the roots of the nitrogen-fixing plants (like peas and beans). While they start off with living in the soil, at some point they attach themselves to plant roots and creates swellings called nodules. From here, they go to work converting gaseous nitrogen locked in the soil's air-spaces into a mineralized form that plants can absorb. Research into the effects of electricity upon bacteria suggests the following:

- Bacteria can be manipulated by electric fields.
- Bacteria can be disseminated underground via electro-osmosis and electrophoresis.
- Electric fields increase bacterial metabolic activity.
- Electric fields accelerate bacterial reproductive cycles.

Microbial Transport Effects

Charged particles which include microorganisms may be affected by two processes:

- Electro-osmosis
- Electrophoresis

Electro-osmosis, if you remember from before, is the mechanism that describes how water, in a porous environment, can be forced to move or flow within an electric field. When water flows in this manner, the movements of positively-charged microbes are also affected, resulting in a net flow of water and microbes in the same direction, towards the negative electrode.

Electrophoresis works in a similar manner and transports negatively charged cells toward the system's anode(-). As such, movement is determined by the electrical charge characteristics of the particular bacterial strain. Thus, the direction of bacterial movement can be controlled by altering the electrical field and its polarity.

In electrical experiments performed by Suni et al.[93], bacterial strains were found to disperse faster when they move via electroosmotic water flows toward the cathode. When comparing migration rates across different soil types, it turns out that bacteria:

- Flows fastest within fine sands (1.0 cm/h)
- Flows at mid-speed in garden soils (0.6cm/h)
- Flows slowest in clays (0.1cm/h)

Changes in Metabolic Activity

In addition to being used for moving microbes around a liquid medium, electric fields have also been found to alter cellular metabolism.

While a significant body of research covers the study of electric fields on microbes, the effects of electrical stimulation can vary

[93](Suni, 2004)

significantly between helpful and harmful. This depends upon the type of bacteria involved and the nature of the electrical stimuli. For example, in a study of alternating current (AC) electric fields on *Lactobacillus acidophilus* during fermentation, a frequency of 60Hz with high-frequency harmonics present was found to cause a significant increase in bacterial growth[94]. On the other hand, in a similar study on AC fields, when the applied voltage is at a much higher level (approximately 6kV or 6000 volts), the result was a decrease in the bacterial population[95]. This realization has become key in the deliberate sterilization of different forms of bacteria for use in food processing and other industries[96].

On a more positive front, a study from the *Chinese Journal of Applied Chemistry* showed that the metabolic activity of *Bacillus subtilis* in a low-voltage DC field was multiplied between 1.9 and 3.8 times over the control when exposed to extremely low amounts of current (on the order of 45 microamps or so)[97].

What are the mechanisms behind these effects?

While certainly more that could be learned, the mechanisms that cause these effects are likely due to a good number of the following:

- Increases in surface hydrophobicity
- Changes in cell shape
- Increases the number of surface extracellular substances
- Increases the negative surface electrostatic charge
- Increases cellular metabolism[98]
- Increases cellular reproduction rate[99]

---

[94](Laleh, Sastry, Yousef 2008)
[95](Hassanein, Ali 2013)
[96](Zvitov, 2004)
[97](Ma, Shengxue 2012)
[98](Wang, 2004)
[99](Wang, 2004)

- Other physiological changes from electrical or other environmental stresses

While the mechanisms and effects are not necessarily well understood, it is known that beneficial effects from electric fields are realized within specific stimulation ranges or windows. It is for this reason that more experimentation is needed in this area so we can learn how to best achieve benefits from electrical stimulation on both fronts: from the metabolic increases for beneficial strains, and from the inhibition or inactivation of harmful strains, like *E. coli*.

It is worth noting that in lab tests where electricity is applied to soil, any cell death that occurs may partially be due to electrolysis reactions that occur on or near the electrodes. These reactions are capable of generating chemical oxidants that could be harmful to bacteria (e.g. chloride ions). Wang et. al. has even found that an electrical current of more than 20 milliAmps can deform or destroy bacterial cells. Later on, this will need to be kept in mind when it comes to designing electroculture systems. In cases where high voltage (in the 1000s of Volts) is applied, the induced currents in the cells are capable of affecting the orientation of membrane lipids and ultimately, cell vitality. They are even capable of directly oxidizing portions of the cell itself[100].

Enhanced Reproductive Activity

It has also been determined that electric fields can also increase the number of microorganisms via enhancements in their reproduction rate while also strengthening their activity. The benefit of these changes is their ability to increase nutrient availability while simultaneously building up organic matter in the soil[101].

---
[100](Luo, Wang, Zhang, Qian 2005)
[101](Wang, 2004)

Stimulation of Aerobic Bacteria

It's worth noting that electricity can induce responses on both aerobic and anaerobic forms of bacteria. Based on the fact that electrolysis reactions in wet soil create oxygen as a by-product, I think that there would be a preferential acceleration of aerobic bacteria. When aerobic bacteria are stimulated, it maximizes their population compared to any anaerobic populations that are present in the soil, thus increasing the plant's ability to convert essential nutrients into a form that is available for uptake. One example is nitrogen. In nitrogen fixation, microbes convert gaseous nitrogen into a form that can be used by plants. Under accelerated microbial conditions, it is possible that greater amounts of gaseous or other forms of nitrogen are able to enter the plant, thus adding to the aforementioned benefits like greener leaves and increased growth[102].

Summary

It can be easily seen that the use of externally-applied electric fields in conjunction with traditional forms of fertilizer (either chemical or organic) can be used to significantly reduce the amount of fertilizer needed. Plants can typically only use a small amount of applied fertilizer since it's not in a form that's readily available. Thus using processes like electroculture can greatly improve fertilizing efficiency. This can result in a significant reduction in the production cost of agricultural activities. The simultaneous improvement of soil conditions that comes about through the action of making larger soil aggregates, increasing water retention and soil oxygenation is another benefit that can be realized as well.

In the next chapter we'll get into the details behind electricity's role

---
[102](Weatherbee, 2011)

upon the physiological make-up of plants.

Chapter 9: Mechanisms of Plant Electrophysiology

The response of biological cells and tissues to electric fields to is known as electrotropism.

Plants are sensitive to many different forms of stimuli. Most people know that plants respond to well-known environmental conditions such as temperature, light quality and direction, as well as moisture. Plants can also respond to lesser-known forms of stimuli as well, like electricity.

As mentioned previously, a number of experimenters over the last few centuries demonstrated how electric fields affect plant growth in both field and lab-based environments. Perhaps they first started experimenting with electricity in an agricultural context when they noticed how well plants grow after a lightning storm. Not only does the air smell fresh and clean, but plants and trees seem to have a quality about them that makes them pop, like they're bursting with new energy. Or perhaps there was an observation made in some part of the earth where there tended to be a greater amount of naturally-occurring electricity flowing through the ground, also creating a rich growing experience for plants. Nonetheless, these researchers successfully replicated the natural electrical phenomena using artificial forms of electricity.

In the observation of both naturally-occurring and generated forms of electricity and their actions on plants, it was seen to affect many physiological aspects of plant biology. Affected parts include:

- Root growth

- Shoot growth
- Flowers: timing, color and aroma
- Fruits: size, maturity, aroma and sweetness
- Stress resistance: water, heat, cold, disease and infestation

At a high level, some of the most significant effects upon plant biology include:

- Metabolic enhancements
- Polarization of cells and tissues
- Nutrient assimilation & uptake improvements
- Activation of growth hormones and latent genetic traits

This section aims to briefly cover, in a somewhat simplified form, some of the specific aspects of plant physiology that relate to the growing of plants with electricity. This is normally a very complex subject that includes knowledge of many closely related fields such as biochemistry, bioelectricity, cell biology and molecular biology. However, by forming a basis of understanding as to why plants respond as they do, it will help with understanding why some of the effects are observed. Furthermore, it will give clues as to how plant growth can be deliberately manipulated for agricultural improvements. It will be left to the reader to research the topics below in a more thorough manner if they would like a more detailed understanding of the mechanisms involved.

Below is a concept map showing a more complete view of the vast number of physiological responses that can be expressed:

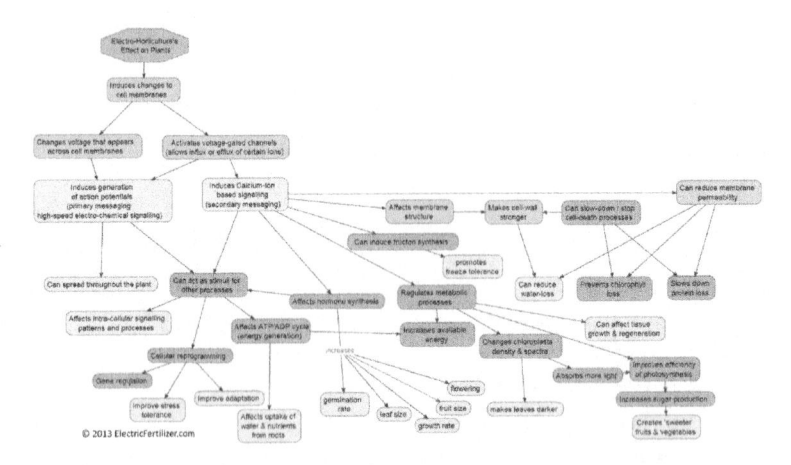

Chapter 9: Mechanisms of Plant Electrophysiology   88

Physiological Effects from Electric Field Stimulation

Let's begin by covering the topic of electrotropism, or how plants respond to electricity from a movement perspective.

Electricity and Polar Cells

Similar to the way that plants grow towards a light source, with electroculture, some plants exhibit a similar response in the way that their roots grow towards or away from electrical sources.

The way this works is there are some plants that have cells with imbalanced charge distributions on them. These are known as "polar cells". Cells of this type tend to have a collection of similar electric charges on only one side of their cellular membrane compared to non-polar cells that more or less have a balanced charge all around them.

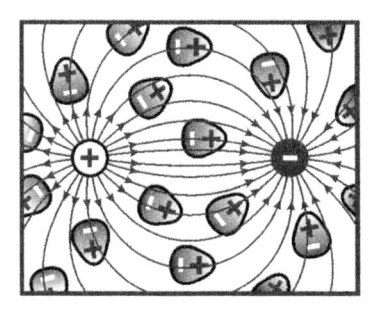

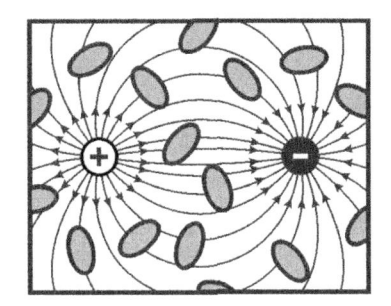

Chapter 9: Mechanisms of Plant Electrophysiology

Polar vs Non-Polar Cells

Source: Universiteit Gent: Liquid Crystal & Photonics Group[103]

They can be found on regular roots as well as root hairs. So, depending upon the species of plant, its root hairs may have a tendency to grow either towards or away from the positive source of the electric field. For example, plants that have roots that tend to grow towards the positive electrode include *Vicia, Zea, Secale, Hordeum, Cannabis, Ricinus, Cucurbita, Tropaeolum, Convolvulus, Cynaria, Helianthus*, and others[104][105].

One of the major contributors to the discovery of these behaviors was Andrew Goldsworthy in collaboration with his colleagues Minas Mina and K.S. Rathore. With Mina, by measuring minute amounts of electrical current that flow into and out of plant cells, they observed that the cells of some plant roots are polar. What this means is that they have a preference that has them responding to an electric field by growing in one particular orientation. For example, if the field was oriented north-south, the portion of root cells called the callus would orient themselves along that axis, with one side of the cell being closer to the north. They also found out that these cells can be effectively 're-programmed' when stronger electric fields were applied to cells in the opposite direction[106].

---
[103]http://lcp.elis.ugent.be/research/electrophoresis
[104](Plowman, 1904)
[105](Ishikawa, 1990)
[106](Goldsworthy)

In addition to affecting the direction of growth, Goldsworthy and Rathore found that for some plants, the flow of current in one direction through the plant (e.g. roots to leaves) stimulated growth while flow in the opposite direction inhibited it. Consider the results as described in an April 9, 1985 New York Times article covering the research:

> "The research workers, K. S. Rathore and A. Goldsworthy of the college's department of pure and applied biology, applied direct current of about a millionth of an ampere to cells of tobacco plants growing in laboratory flasks. The specimens were growing as aggregations of cells called callus rather than as complete plants." The influence of electric current on these cell cultures first became noticeable after about 10 days and was dramatically obvious by 22 days. "The effect was dependent on the direction of the current," the scientists reported. "When the callus was made negative, the growth rate was stimulated by about 70 percent, whereas current in the reverse direction was slightly inhibitory.[107]"

One possible explanation as to why plants would behave in this manner may be so they can align themselves with naturally-occurring[108] ground currents.

While the number of interactions taking place underground is staggering, especially considering all of the organic and inorganic chemical compounds, soil fungi, and bacterial strains that could be involved with each other, perhaps the plant's ability to generate and respond to electric fields is part of the underlying mechanics behind the formation of beneficial plant communities. For instance, in plant communities or guilds there may be a relationship between one set of plants creating electric fields in their roots that influence

---
[107](NY Times, 1985)
[108]In case you missed it earlier, naturally-occurring ground currents are also known as telluric currents.

surrounding plants in a way that helps draw in not only substances exuded from the others' roots but may also help direct the movement of other plants' roots either towards or away from them. In truth, there are tons of hidden layers in the inter-relationships between all life, the planet Earth, and the Universe itself that we are so far away from understanding at this time. The fact that plants respond to electric fields may be yet another 'sensor' by which plants respond to their surroundings and to their micro and macro-based environments.

Electrophysiological Effects

There are three main ways that plants respond to and interact with electric fields:

- Cell membranes interactions
- Electrical signaling
- Electrochemical signaling

We'll start with covering the electrical effects first, and then later, go into the electrochemical effects, even though there will be bleed-over between the methods.

The predominant way that plants know how to respond to any stimuli, including that of external electromagnetic fields, is through the plants' internal communications network. This 'network', which consists of both chemical and electrical signaling methods, controls the flow of information within the plant's entire body and beyond[109]. It uses these signals to respond to sources of internal and external stimuli which can range from the detection of chemical compounds in the soil such as root exudates[110], to the activation of

---

[109] As we'll see later in Chapters 11 & 12, researchers have now shown that there are inter-plant communications that take place in response to external stimuli (like insect attack) via pheromones or volatile chemical compounds.

[110] Various substances that are released into the soil from roots.

various hormones or genes which could tell the plant to initiate certain behaviors. For instance, hormones could be activated in response to stressors such as insect attack, where the production of "insect repellent" chemical compounds would be synthesized. Under normal conditions this reaction may occur, but under stimulation, reports so far indicate that plants begin to take actions for actively repelling insects, perhaps through the amplifying the original responses.

Electricity in Biology

In this day and age it's common knowledge that both humans and animals are electrical in nature. Part of the reason this is universally known is because of the progress made in the biomedical engineering community. Through their efforts, devices are now commonly found within the medical community like electrocardiograms (ECGs) and electroencephalograms (EEGs)[111]. We know that even fish and insects are electrical. Electric eels are capable of delivering electric shocks to subdue other fish, and fireflies electrochemically blink on and off in the early evenings of summer. Even with this knowledge, how often do we think of plants as electrical, too?

Because of many of the same mechanisms that exist in mammals, fish, and insects, plants are also electrical in nature. How is that so? What these two different forms of life have in common are their cell-based makeup. Cells are electrical by their very nature due to a wide range of complex interactions that occur between electrically-charged atoms, molecules, proteins and other structures. These interactions can be described using concepts from cell biology and electro-chemistry.

Unstable atoms[112], called ions, are constantly flowing into and out

---

[111]ECGs measure the electrical signals around a beating heart and EEGs measure those coming from the brain.
[112]Unstable because they are missing or have extra valence electrons.

Chapter 9: Mechanisms of Plant Electrophysiology 93

of cells due to the constant state of change that occurs inside, outside and between cells. This flow of ions can be found traversing the fluids that surround cells (known as extracellular fluid) and the fluids inside the cell (known as the cytoplasm) via the cell's outer membrane as well as the different organs and structures found within it. The ebb and flow of ionic uptake, processing and release that occur in response to the happenings within and around all cells, causes an unequal distribution of ions[113] across the cell's plasma membrane, forming one of the mechanisms that creates electric fields in basic cell biology.

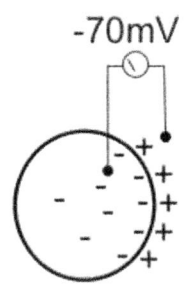

Cells are Electrical! Illustration of a Cell Having a Net Negative Charge

Goldsworthy also made significant progress in developing theories as to what happens electrically within the cellular structures of plants. He knew that the flow of ions across cells was akin to the flow of electrons moving through a wire, creating what we know as electrical current. In this, he thought that they played a major role in plant development[114].

Taking the ionic flows discussed above to a deeper level of understanding, let's begin by discussing how voltage and current relate to cells. First, the difference in ionic concentrations across a barrier such as a cell membrane is called an electrochemical gradient, also known as a membrane potential. An electric field gets established between both sides of the barrier when there is a difference in ionic

---
[113] Known as a concentration gradient.
[114] (Goldsworthy,Volkov, 2006)

concentrations. If there aren't any differences, then it is said that there is no membrane potential (or the membrane voltage is zero) because everything is in equilibrium.

When electric fields are present, which are most of the time since a cell is rarely, if ever, in equilibrium with its environment, they play a major role in the operation and upkeep of plant biology. They do so by having a critical role in the creation of electrical or chemical-based signals used throughout the plant. Scientists like Goldsworthy and his research associates have suggested that these signals are used in the communications of messages not only within a single cell, but also across many multiples of cells. In fact, they have experimentally determined that fluctuating cellular electric fields can cause signals to spread throughout the entire plant[115]. This will be discussed in more detail shortly.

Marinesco[116], a French biochemist, found that the flow of ions in the plants' capillary systems can produce electricity, too. In one experiment, he measured the voltage between the roots of a plant and a point in the stem just above ground level. He found the voltage to be approximately 0.4 volts. Thus voltages can be found not only across cell boundaries, but also any location along the flow of ionic substances within a plant. It's interesting today that experimenters are starting to even look at plants as living batteries for powering remotely located devices, in lieu of using solar panels.

In the following section, we'll explore some of the ways that electrochemical signals are created and transmitted throughout the plant. Then, the wide array of possible effects that can be activated through these mechanisms will be discussed. We'll begin by exploring how electric fields influence cell membranes and the flow of ions.

---
[115](Goldsworthy,Volkov, 2006)
[116](Dorchester, 1937; p9)

The Cell Membrane

As we covered before, the 'cell membrane' is effectively a wall that keeps all operating portions of the cell self-contained, separated from their external environment. Electrochemical signals and nutrients are able to pass through this barrier by receptors and protein transport structures embedded within the membrane.

Technically, the membrane isn't a solid wall; it is actually a wall that can selectively allow some substances to pass through it while blocking others (known as a permeable membrane). Gases such as oxygen and carbon dioxide can pass relatively freely through these membranes using simple diffusion, while water, inorganic ions (e.g. sodium, calcium, potassium), and more complex metabolites (e.g. amino acids, antioxidants, and vitamins) cannot. In simple diffusion, the cell wall acts like a simple balance in the form of a pressure valve, striving to keep chemical equilibrium by allowing the materials in excess on one side of the boundary to only pass while blocking the flow of substances in the opposite direction. Diffusion can be visualized by thinking about how a drop of ink placed into a glass of water will eventually spread from a concentrated drop to form a uniformly colored solution.

To transport larger, complex, or charged materials across the cell membrane, two other types of methods are used:

Passive transport[117] * Simple diffusion * Channel proteins * Carrier proteins Active transport * Ion pumps

---

[117] Passive Transport allows the movement of uncharged or small particles through the cell membrane without any energy expenditure.

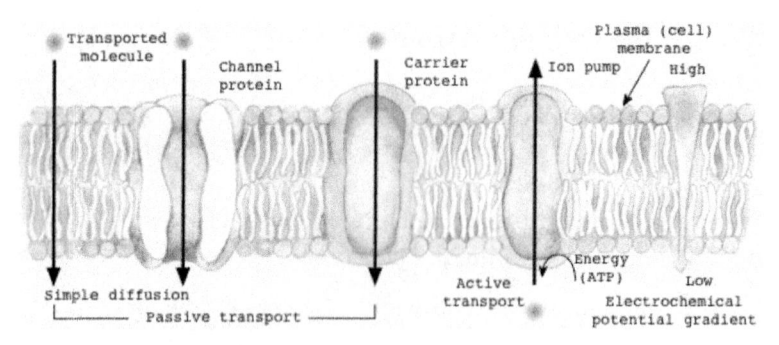

Cell Membrane Transport Mechanisms

Source: Based on (Taiz, 2002)

Passive Transport

Passive transport, or the transport of materials across the cell boundary from an area of high concentration to an area of low concentration, can be accomplished via simple diffusion (described above), or using a method called facilitated diffusion that occurs via transport proteins embedded within the cell membrane.

In facilitated-diffusion, protein structures called channel or carrier proteins are used to facilitate transport across the membrane. These proteins, also called voltage-gated channels, can handle not only individual ions, but larger molecules as well. Furthermore, they act as voltage sensors in that they change shape is response to electrical signals. This change in shape is what enables the passage of complex molecules to flow through them.

> In fact, I would say that it's this one particular physiological organ, the voltage-gated channel, that is the reason why electroculture works. It is the enabling response that ultimately leads to chain reactions that bring about beneficial changes throughout the plant.

Note that portions of the membrane are permeable to only a subset of all of the possible ions that may be available in its environment,

Chapter 9: Mechanisms of Plant Electrophysiology   97

e.g. potassium ions or chloride ions. The cell membrane acts as a gatekeeper. These channel proteins are capable of selectively allowing (via substance-level detectors or voltage-control signals) some substances to enter while simultaneously excluding others. They respond not only to chemical signals, but also electrical ones as well that specify which ions are allowed to pass. Once the protein is told to pass a certain type of substance, it can allow a very large volume of it to pass through.

Cell membranes can have varying degrees of electric potential between their internal and external portions. Whenever there is a membrane potential, which in this case occurs from a buildup of similarly charged atoms and molecules on one side or the other, the result is a flow of electric charge if the barriers are open. So, when electrical current is blocked in some way, a voltage (also known as potential difference) builds up across the blocking element and the relative portions of the cell wall.

> Similar to the voltage difference that can be measured across two different parts of a circuit, in biology, the differences in charge across the cell boundary can be measured as an electric potential difference.

Keep in mind that when large amounts of charged nutrients are allowed into the cell, the net effect of their movement will result in a flow of electrical current and a change in the induced voltage as well. This is a very important point in that the changing of electrical potential across the cell boundary can bring about major physiological effects. This will be covered in detail, shortly.

Active Transport

Plants need to take in nutrients from the soil in order to grow, and since plants are a living container of many forms of nutrients, the concentration of nutrients within their cellular structure is naturally much higher than that of the soil. Since diffusion only works by moving substances from an area of high concentration to a lower one, it isn't a suitable method for shuttling nutrients from the soil into the cellular structure of the plant. To get around this, active transport mechanisms are used. These mechanisms are also used in other physiological operations of the plant ranging from the delivery of sucrose that's produced by photosynthesis, to the recharging or refractory period of the cell after a whole-plant signaling event called an action potential.

To facilitate the transfer of charged substances into and out of cells against an established concentration or electrical gradient, a different type of protein structure called an ion pump is used. Situated throughout the cell wall, this type of protein requires energy in the form of ATP to move ions "upstream" against the established concentration gradient[118].

Since ion pumps require energy in order to operate, as noted above, keep in mind that once sugars are created by photosynthesis, their dispersal throughout the plant also requires the use of energy. This is an important fact that should be noted with respect to using electro-horticulture methods for extended periods of time; that is, it may be best for electrical stimulation systems to only be active during daylight hours, when a plant can create more of the energy it needs. However, since energy is also created during the plant's respiration cycle, which occurs at night, this may be less of an issue. More on this topic will be covered later in Chapter 13's section on system design.

Electrical Signaling

As we now know, biological systems are inherently electrical in their cellular makeup. Plants and other higher organisms use

---
[118](Schroeder, 1999)

electrical and chemical communication signals to control a wide variety of biological processes including hormone synthesis, gene expression and various metabolic processes[119]. In the following two sections we will cover the basics of electrical and chemical signaling. Knowing how cells communicate with each other will give insight into how externally-induced electric fields affect a myriad of subsystems found within plant life.

To start with an example: If a plant is under some form of stress, e.g., stress from not having enough water, a number of events are triggered that may cause a plant genetically tuned to the condition to respond in a protective manner. As will be explained in the sections that follow, the stimuli of water-stress is sensed by various cells within the plant. This will subsequently cause the emission of a series of communications signals that are broadcast to the rest of the plant. Depending upon the type of signal, its strength, and other factors, a number of physiological responses may be triggered, e.g. the synthesis of ethylene which bolsters the cell walls against fluid leakage. Plants that are able to survive dry weather conditions for extended periods may develop a special form of tolerance to these conditions and even pass them on to their offspring. Since the development of genetic adaptations is linked to how plants are stimulated throughout its life, the plants' electrical environment (whether natural or artificial) also plays a role.

From an electrical point of view, there are a number of signaling modes that are triggered by different forms and degrees of stimuli. These broadly include:

- Action potentials
- Variation potentials
- Transient voltages
- Voltage spikes
- Electrochemical voltage gradients

---
[119](Goldsworthy,Volkov, 2006)

Since most research to date has discovered that the primary response to external electrical fields is in the generation of signals called action potentials (AP), that will be the topic of focus in this book.

What are Action Potentials?

Action potentials can be imagined to be a burst of electrical activity that, once activated, are capable of traveling throughout the plant. As they work their way through the plant's biological makeup, they have the ability to initiate a wide range of physiological responses, including those affecting growth, nutrient uptake, reproduction, defense and others. Being that so many aspects of plant growth are affected by this internal form of electricity, it makes sense that they form the major basis of the physiological effects realized by plants when they're subjected to external stimulation.

In essence, APs are a form of electrical signaling that takes place in cells that are capable of being excited. Note that some cells are excitable and others are not. The cells that are excitable can produce an AP signal only if certain electrochemical conditions are met. The emitted signal itself is a high voltage pulse, or firing that is capable of spreading far and wide throughout the plant. They are often found to be one of the main mechanisms behind the way plants react to various forms of stimuli including:

- Touch response, e.g. Venus Fly Trap (*Dionaea muscipula*)
- Reacting to chemical compound in the soil, e.g. root exudates of nearby plants
- Insect infestation, e.g. aphids
- Phototropism, i.e. light stimulus
- Pollination events

AP Generation

Compressing the Spring[120]

Under normal circumstances, the flow of ions into and out of a cell are generally equal. This means that for all of the inflows of nutrients, there are equal outflows of waste or reaction products that go back into the extracellular fluid surrounding the cells.

The chemical concentrations on both sides of the cell tend to be in equilibrium over time. Electrically, due to the normal operational nature of the active transport proteins, cells tend to favor an electronegative state. What this means is that these ion pumps often push a larger number of positive charges (like calcium, Ca^{2+}) outside of the cell compared to the ones that they take in, thus keeping the cell slightly more negatively charged. The effect of this is that it's like compressing a spring, causing its potential energy to build up over time. As larger amounts of positive charges build up around the cell wall, negative charges accumulate on the inside of the cell walls. At this point, the cell is said to be in a state called the negative membrane resting potential, and is measured from the inside of the cell to the outside[121]. This build up of membrane potential (typically about -70 milliVolts) is what's needed to prepare the cell for the creation of a signaling event known as an action potential[122].

Releasing the Spring

When some form of stimuli is sensed, usually by sensitive receptors that are located throughout the outward-facing surface of the cell membrane, they create a change in the voltage on some of the transport proteins. These transport proteins, also known as voltage-gated channels (VGCs), can be electrically controlled; therefore, they can be programmed to open and close in response to changes in voltage, similar to the way an electromechanical relay works

---

[120]Note: To help with visualizing the generation of APs, we'll throw in some references of using a mechanical 'spring' to show how an AP is created.

[121](Goldsworthy; Volkov and Jovanov 2002; Lautner et al. 2005)

[122](Goldsworthy; Volkov)

like the one in your car door (controlling the door locks). A small amount of control voltage (e.g. from the switch) is used to control the flow of a larger amount of current (e.g. the current needed to move the door locks). When the ionic charge levels meet a certain threshold voltage, also known as an amplitude window[123], they cause the various VGCs to change state. The reason the term amplitude window is used is because it represents a range of amplitudes, or voltage levels that may be what's needed to open the ion channels, all depending upon the type of ion channel, the tissue type and the plant species.

Once the receptors are sufficiently stimulated, they cause the channel proteins to open up, letting calcium ions in from the cell's extracellular fluid. Since cells are normally operating in a negative charge environment, when the gates open, a flood of positive ions enters the cell's interior - not only because there is a buildup of charge concentration on the outside near the gate, but also because like-charges repel each other. These repelling charges then push each other away, into the channel protein, and out of the other side, into the cell. So, when these charges flood into the cell, it changes the amount of calcium concentration within the cell. The amount of change, as well it's location within the cell, has an effect on the response[124]. Differences in calcium levels are called calcium signatures[125] and play a part in the physiological response mechanism of the plant.

---

[123] Home Page of Dr. A. Goldsworthy
[124] (Hepler, 2005; p.5)
[125] (Tuteja, Narendra, and Mahajan, p1)

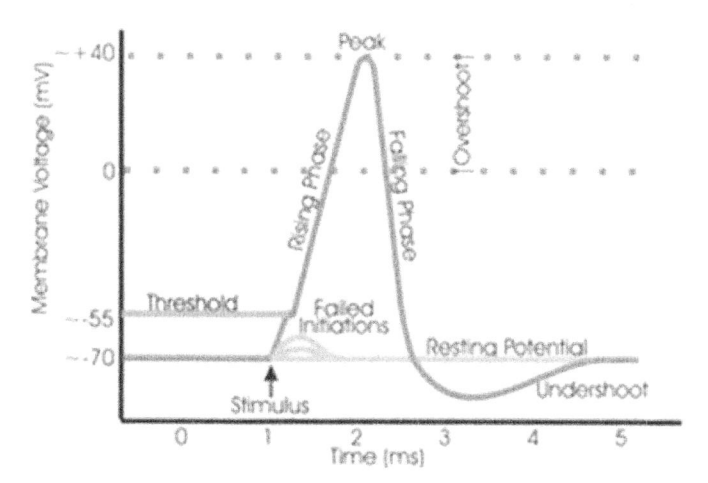

Chapter 9: Mechanisms of Plant Electrophysiology   103

Schematic Illustration of an Action Potential

Source: Wikipedia[126]

Once inside, this mass of positive charge spreads about[127] and causes what's called cellular depolarization, or a reversal of the polarity within the cell. At first the cell's interior was slightly negative. Now that the floodgates have been opened, the interior of the cell starts to experience a huge increase in positive charge (a voltage spike). If the amount of the voltage is greater than a certain threshold (the depolarization limit), then the spike will hit a peak value called the "action potential". Note that once the limit has been reached, any increases in the voltage level will have no additional effect on the response. It simply causes the voltage spike to fire.

This all-or-none type of response is indicative of typical AP behavior. It's like pressing a needle against a piece of rubber. Until you penetrate the rubber, you can keep pushing it but once the rubber is penetrated, that is it. You might push the needle further but nothing dramatic will happen[128]. To assign a number to these voltages, in some plants, the membrane depolarization level can reach upwards

---
[126] http://en.wikipedia.org/wiki/Action_potential
[127] Known as electrotonic potential
[128] (Saito, 2012)

of +100 mV[129].

Propagation

Now that we covered how APs are generated, let's go into how they spread. After the membrane depolarization event occurs which causes a voltage spike, a massive exodus of calcium ions (positive charges) flows back into the surrounding environment triggering more VGCs to open up on the surrounding cells. It is in this way that the AP and the flood of calcium ions cause a chain-reaction that spreads these signals to surrounding cells, that if are also excitable, will spread far and wide, possibly throughout the entire plant.

It is for this reason that action potentials have been suggested as being information carriers[130] capable of relaying electrical signals throughout most of the plant. By facilitating high-speed message or information transfer, it helps the plant react in a timely manner in response to most forms of internally or externally-triggered stimuli[131].

Electrochemical Signaling

In addition to AP-based signaling, there are also chemical information carriers that can relay information from one portion of the plant to another. In the next section we're going to focus on the role of calcium as a regulator of plant physiological processes.

The Role of Calcium in Plant Biology

To start, as you may recall from earlier, the massive release of calcium after each AP 'pulse' causes waves of calcium ions to

---
[129]In *Dionaea muscipula*; See (DuBois, 2010) for more details.
[130](Goldsworthy,Volkov, 2006)
[131](ESA Report, 2008)

spread throughout the plant via each cell cluster that the calcium ions come in contact with. What is the effect of this?

Alberto Lagoa, research assistant to Goldsworthy, found that his tissue cultures became greener when weak electric currents were passed through them, suggesting that the calcium uptake was increasing their growth by acting as a secondary messenger. He also suggested that this may be the reason why gardens tend to look particularly lush and green after a thunderstorm[132]. As a secondary messenger that switches on the enzymes within cells, calcium could be another major reason behind the wide range of effects that tend to occur with electrical stimulation. Goldsworthy described the mechanism in a statement as follows:

> "Calcium ions bound to the surfaces of cell membranes are important in maintaining their stability. They help hold together the phospholipid molecules that are an essential part of their make-up. Without these ions, cell membranes are weakened and are more likely to tear under the stresses and strains imposed by the moving cell contents (these membranes are only two molecules thick!).... Calcium also controls the rate of many metabolic processes.[133]"

More details of how calcium affects physiological responses in the plant will be covered in the next chapter.

Caveats of AP and Calcium-based Electrochemical Responses

One last point on the topic of APs and calcium signaling: there are some caveats to be concerned with since it's possible that too much

---
[132](Young, 1997)
[133](Chopra,Formitchev-Zamilov)

calcium can enter the cell during the membrane depolarization phase. Depending upon the state of a cell, if there is too great of an increase in calcium levels, Goldsworthy suggests that the possibility exists for the cell to be driven into a state of stress, capable of causing serious damage to the cell membranes. He also states that the overall physiological state of the plant itself is important, too. If the plant is in a state of stress due to lack of water or nutrients, then once the AP is generated, the cell can be impaired in its ability to remove the surplus calcium. This type of response will likely adversely affect the health of the plant, possibly having lethal effects[134]. This notion of plants having the potential for experiencing an electrical overdose has also been discovered by the prominent physicist and plant physiologist from India, J.C. Bose.

Goldsworthy also notes that AP chain reactions (also called enzyme cascades) are dependent on plant species and tissue type as they both have different enzymatic chains available for activation. In other words, what works for one type of plant or tissue may not work on another type. It is therefore suggested that plants and tissues may have differing "calcium signatures" that are not the same across all plant life[135].

One last reason why improved calcium signaling can cause problems in certain plants is due to the effect of "calcium memory". This is a phenomena that occurs when plants stop responding due to being overstimulated in either amount or duration[136]. This is akin to getting into a state of sensory overload where a person's nervous system gets fried from over-stimulation. In plants, this calcium over-stimulation can cause a lack of responsiveness due to the plant's need for a mandatory rest period of several minutes to several hours.

Thus, in terms of an electroculture-based growing system, it may

---
[134](Tuteja, Narendra, and Mahajan,p4)
[135](Tuteja, Narendra, and Mahajan,p4)
[136](Tuteja, Narendra, and Mahajan,p4; Knight et al. (1996).34))

be necessary to allow plants to rest from stimulation, whether it's an overnight resting period or many smaller rest periods spaced throughout the day. Of course this would be a species-dependent issue, where for one set of plants a longer resting period may be needed over another set. This is an area of electroculture research that has yet to be explored in terms of maximizing efficiency.

It is also worth noting that this may provide a possible explanation as to why some of the early researchers[137] in the field of electroculture had mixed results, especially over long periods of time. Being overstimulated may have put too much of a strain on many of the plants that were experimented upon back in the 1770s-1930s. In addition, they may have been trying the same exact protocols on the same plants which simply respond differently because they are different. If the seeds were saved and were used in the next generation of planting, it's also conceivable that the plants had a memory of how much stimulation they were capable of receiving, and were possible more easily over-stimulated.

On the other hand, since earth batteries were one of the most prevalent power sources of the day, the problems that eventually caused the disbanding of the Committee may have come about through problems with zinc soil toxicity, caused by many years of running the same experiments on the same plots of land. In Chapter 13, covering system design, we'll share some new practices that will help you avoid some of the shortcomings that plagued experiments of the past.

Summary

By gaining a basic understanding of the fundamentals of soil science, electrochemistry, and plant physiology, one can start to understand how the application of electric fields to soils and to

---

[137] Notably, those from the mid-1930s like the UK Electro-Culture Committee of the Ministry of Agriculture and Fisheries. Read more about it here.

plants can bring about significant changes. These changes are real, and understanding the mechanisms and processes involved will not only help with the underlying comprehension of what's going on, but will help the reader in their use and experimentation with electroculture. In the next chapter, the background knowledge just covered will help you with understanding the many discovered benefits from the application of electro-horticultural methods.

Chapter 10: The Effects of Electroculture on Plants

In this chapter, we will be covering the more interesting side of plant physiology - the large-scale effects that can be observed during electrical stimulation. As we mentioned in the last chapter, a wide number of physiological effects can be induced through APs and calcium signaling processes due to the feedback or amplification factor that occurs as these mechanisms interact with each other. The result of all of this activity is the creation of a superhighway of electrical and chemical messages that flow throughout the plant. As we learned, these messages are capable of causing a great number of things to happen. In fact, Reddy and Reddy[138] have found:

> "...there are approx. 700 known protein components that function at various stages of calcium signaling. These have yet to be identified and characterized."

Thus, when plants are exposed to external electric fields, what follows is a huge increase in activity. Considering that just from the calcium signaling process alone that there are hundreds of protein components, each responsible for controlling different portions of the plant's physiology, the range of effects is probably larger than we can imagine at this time. Since proteins represent functions codified by the genetics involved, depending on the particular plant's DNA[139], its environment and its history of dealing with past stressors, many different outcomes are possible.

---
[138] (Hepler, 2005; ref: Reddy and Reddy (2004))
[139] i.e. genetic makeup

Let's go deeper and start exploring the range of physiological responses that are possible via the previous concept-map from chapter 9.

Genetic Responses

Genetics, or the study of biological characteristics and how they are projected into future generations, is one of the major areas of plant physiology that can be affected by external forces. These characteristics, codified within strands of DNA, represent cellular information that can be transformed into different functional or structural forms. Some traits or functions that can be affected by the use of electric fields are:

- Budding amount and timing
- Flowering timing
- Disease resistance
- Salt tolerance
- Drought tolerance
- Freeze tolerance

Most growers, especially those working in the genetic sciences or those comfortable with the idea of GMOs, would find the ability to tweak these particular traits to be very desirable. What if there were a way to bring forth these qualities without going through generations of successive breeding or direct genetic manipulation? With electroculture, this is a possibility.

In this section we are going to very briefly touch on the basics of microbiological genetics as it relates to electro-horticulture and then move forward into the other effects that may occur.

A High Level Primer

Let's start by talking briefly about how DNA works at a high level. Genes, or segments of DNA, are molecular encodings that represent each and every aspect of a plant's innate developmental and functional characteristics. Composed of various combinations or sequences of chemical structures, genetic information within DNA strands undergo a series of manipulations that allow them to express themselves into functional units. This occurs via a three-step process:

1- Replication 2- Transcription 3- Translation

Replication is exactly what it sounds like: a duplication process.

Transcription is not so easy to describe. It refers to the process of transferring genetic code within DNA into another molecular form called RNA. RNA refers to a set of biological molecules that perform a number of vital roles within cells, like protein synthesis or perhaps acting as the sensing or cellular communication controllers.

The last step, translation, refers to the protein synthesis role. As we covered earlier, one functional use of proteins is their ability to control the flow of nutrients into and out of cells (using ion pumps and other regulatory proteins). Depending upon the type of protein that's synthesized, they can do much more - such as becoming structural members, performing metabolic regulation and immunity functions, and acting as communications agents that responding to stimuli.

Even though it's a complex cycle, one can begin to see how electricity can potentially cause chain reactions throughout an entire plant...because everything is connected!

Over time, scientists have found that plant genetics can be affected by external stimuli. While most botanists are familiar with the concept of adaptability from naturally occurring stressors, comparatively little is known about the effects of electric field stimulation. As shown in the diagram in Chapter 9, a large number of responses are genetic in nature, so let's start by zooming in on the concept map, focusing on the items having to do with genetics.

The Effect of Electrical Stimulation on DNA

The way that electrical stimulation affects plant genetics is in the way that genes express themselves. Gene expression[140], as defined online, is the "conversion of the information encoded in a gene first into messenger RNA and then to a protein."

As we covered in the previous chapter, electrical stimulation affects the way signaling messages are emitted by cells. The responses that can be realized differ depending upon the "signature," or the specific messaging characteristics that are inherent in the messages. By tweaking the amplitude, frequency, timing, duration and other characteristics, different effects may be seen. Thus, depending upon the information transmitted within the signature, different biological components, or in this case, different protein structures can be affected. With the potentially enormous effects that are possible, many of the above benefits could be realized.

Below is a high-level diagram depicting the protein synthesis and their role plant biology.

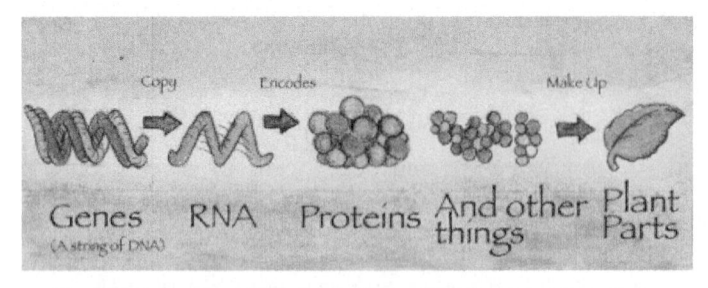

How DNA Becomes Protein and Then Changes into Plant Parts

---

[140] http://wordnetweb.princeton.edu/perl/webwn?s=gene%20expression

Source: Based on Zina Deretsky / National Science Foundation via dana-farber.org[141]

> For a great visual of the many forms that protein can take, check out the Protein Data Bank[142]

By and all, these proteins account for the essentials that plants need to not only function, but to survive and thrive as well. Since all of these proteins (and other structures affected by genetics) can potentially be affected by electric fields, amazing changes and effects can be realized.

Let's move on to cover the other aspects of plant physiology that are affected.

Metabolism

By correlating the interactions between electric fields and their influence over gene expression, scientists have made interesting discoveries. For instance, in one paper[143], the authors surmise that when plants are subjected to an electric field, genes are activated that promote an increase in metabolic activity. While the increase is most likely due to the action potential cycle covered in the previous chapter, there can be other contributing factors as well. The acceleration of a plant's metabolic rate can be observed in two main ways:

1) Monitoring the plant's respiration and transpiration rates. 2) Observing the rate of proton (H+) release from plant roots[144].

---

[141] http://www.dana-farber.org/Newsroom/News-Releases/First-large-scale-map-of-a-plant-s-protein-network-addresses-evolution,-disease-process.aspx
[142] http://www.rcsb.org/pdb/education_discussion/molecule_of_the_month/poster_quickref.pdf
[143] (Chopra,Formitchev-Zamilov)
[144] (Takamura, 2006)

Measuring Respiration

As covered previously, increases in metabolism are correlated with similar increases in respiration rate. The breathing cycle is used in the generation of ATP or cellular energy. At the same time, ATP enables the acceleration of metabolic activity through the powering of protein pumps embedded in the cell membranes. This adds energy to the system, keeping things going by increasing the amount of ionic current flow into the cell. Since this process results in the creation of action potentials, it acts like a positive feedback loop that has the potential of continuing on and on for long periods of time. From my studies of others' experiments as well as my own, I've seen that only minute amounts of stimulation are required to keep the process going for extended periods.

These acceleration effects commonly occur in nature. For instance, after a lightning storm, long after the high-voltage electric fields have dissipated, plants tend to retain their "glow" for a long period of time, making plants seem more vibrant and green. The formation of APs can take a long time to eventually recede, thus being capable of causing subsequent responses and additional AP cycles. This positive feedback loop is probably the mechanism that sustains the initial acceleration effects until long after the stimulation has subsided.

Since both of these processes are interconnected, by monitoring the respiration rate indirectly via transpiration and water loss measurements, changes in metabolic activity can be directly inferred.

Measuring Proton Emissions

For the next method, researchers Tsutomu Takamura and others[145] found a relationship between externally-applied electric fields and the synthesis and consumption of ATP. They found that ATP is consumed in direct proportion to the rate of metabolic activity by way of the ion pumping mechanisms covered in the previous chapter. A side effect of the ion pumping process is that protons get

---

[145] See bibliographic references.

released as specific nutrients are allowed into the cell (e.g. calcium). If you remember how ion pumps work, you'll recall that they allow for the transfer of substances external to the cell into the interior while simultaneously transporting other ions (e.g. hydrogen ions) outwards.

By using a chemical dye, in this case a pH indicator reagent, proton release can be visually "illuminated", illustrating the uptake of nutrients. Greater amounts of protons found around plant roots correlate to larger amounts of uptake, correlating to an increase in metabolic activity. On our resources[146] page we have a link to some studies with pictures and directions on how you perform this study yourself.

This effect has also been observed in Goldsworthy's research where significant and noticeable effects were shown, not only upon the plant's metabolic processes, but regulatory ones as well. Since the ways that genes express themselves are affected by electric fields, it follows suit that these changes would affect hormone synthesis as well. Subsequently, metabolic activity isn't completely reliant on action potential generation alone, but also by the way that the entire plant responds to the generation and transport of hormones.

---

[146] http://ElectricFertilizer.com/book-landing/

🔑 Since plants can produce ATP as an energy source during the day or night, electroculture systems can be run 24 hours a day for a maximum speed advantage. During the day, energy in the form of ATP is created via photosynthesis and stored in sugar molecules. At night, via the process of respiration, ATP is produced when energy is released from sugar.

Yet, while it's possible that these systems can be run all the time, it may not be the best course of action over the long term. Since normally only a small portion of the light energy from photosynthesis goes towards creating sugars to be used at night, it is feasible that the system can eventually run out of energy stores. Stimulated plants work somewhat differently. They increase their light-capturing efficiencies by becoming a darker green in color, which has the effect of increasing their stores beyond normal.

Since it's possible that certain plants may not respond with the extra-greening response, it should be noted that if a plant under stimulation doesn't get darker in color over time, then it may be best to design your electroculture systems to operate more during the daytime compared to the night to minimize stress from energy-depletion.

As shown above, metabolic acceleration can have secondary effects that can affect many parts of the plant's physiology. Here are the systems that can be affected:

- Whole plant growth and regeneration
- Growth and regeneration of tissue cultures
- Generation of chlorophyll and chloroplasts
- Synthesis of sugars, proteins and hormones
- Plant respiration and transpiration processes

Growth Hormones

Hormone synthesis is another major factor that can be affected by the ways that genes express themselves. For those unfamiliar with the function of hormones, they are essentially chemicals that promote and influence cell growth, tissue growth and differentiation. Vital to plant growth, they regulate which tissues grow and when, affecting leaves, stems, fruits and other organs. It is also well established that plant hormones play an essential role in the regulation of signaling pathways. These pathways, on which the aforementioned electrical and electrochemical signals move, are involved in the triggering of plant stress responses.

> Electro-Horticulture follows organic practices, enabling growth hormone-based improvements to occur biologically, rather than through the use of artificially produced chemicals.

It is common in the agricultural sciences that derived and synthetic hormones are used on plants and fruits to serve a number of purposes.

The most important hormones in plant growth and development are:

- Auxins
- Ethylene
- Gibberellins
- Cytokinins
- Brassinosteroids

Let's briefly cover the functions of the most notable ones:

Auxins

The first set of hormones most significant to electroculture are called auxins. These belong to a group of compounds that have an influence on cell enlargement, stem growth, root initiation, bud formation and flowering. They are also known to assist and promote the production of other hormones. For example, regarding their influence on cytokinins, they together control the growth of stems, roots, fruits and help with flowering[147]. In their support of cell enlargement and stem growth, this is accomplished by improving the plasticity of the cell wall, in other words, it improves plants ability to stretch out when cells fill with water.

It is well known that yield increases are one of the effects of electrostimulation. While other growth hormones are also known for boosting growth[148], auxins are likely the source behind yield increases. Normally, growers who look to manipulate the crop yields or size of fruit use synthetic auxins or gibberellins to achieve these goals. With electroculture, these goals can be realized in a much more natural manner.

Gibberellins

The second class of hormones, known to regulate growth and developmental processes including stem elongation, germination, flowering, and others are called gibberellins. In the grape industry, they are used to increase fruit size by enhancing the import of carbohydrates into the developing fruit. They are used extensively to boost the growth of a number of commercial crops including cherries, sugar cane, citrus crops and Golden Delicious apples.

One set of researchers who observed these effects is in Okumura et. al.[149]. They showed in 2006 that the application of direct current

---
[147](Osborne, McManus, 2005)
[148](Podlesny et al., 2005)
[149](Okumura, Muramoto, Shimizu)

fields to plant roots results in an increase in germination rate, changes to plant weight and increases in sprout length. Often thought to be the hormone at work behind the scenes, gibberellin has been known to encourage stem elongation by absorbing additional amounts of water[150]. On the other hand, it is worth noting that different research studies state that the effect of weight gain is often highly dependent on the species being examined. In these cases, weight gain may primarily be due to "water weight" and in others it may be due to the accelerated growth of new tissue.

Ethylene

Lastly, as a part of the generation of action potentials, comes the plant-based manufacture of a more commonly known hormone, ethylene. Through chains of biochemical reactions that take place in response to an increased amount of signaling, the rate of ethylene production is also accelerated. This one has its own set of beneficial effects including[151]:

- Increased rate of plant maturation[152]
- Induced seed ripening
- Induced root hair growth
- Enhanced ripening of fruit[153]
- Enhanced initiation of budding and flowering
- Activation of genetically-programmed events

As shown above, growth hormones can be electrochemically stimulated into being both synthesized and transported throughout the plant. The result is an accumulation of physiological improvements, building upon previously discussed metabolic and genetic

---
[150](Okumura, Muramoto, Shimizu)
[151](Goldsworthy; ref: Davies and Stankovic 2006)
[152](Podlesny et al 2005) via Jain
[153](Boe and Salunkhe 1963) via Jain

processes. Electroculture is a way that plants can be tweaked to self-induce the synthesis of growth hormones. This then becomes a viable alternative for those who are looking to boost their crop output, organically.

Increased Number of Roots

While plants absorb nutrients, chemicals and water via gases and liquids that enter through leaves, roots are the primary organ of nutritional uptake. Plant roots are also used in anchoring the plant to the soil, providing a place for food storage, and inter-plant communications by way of chemical messages that come from other plants (via root exudates).

In a study of the way electric fields act upon plant roots under laboratory conditions, Takamura[154] found that the number of lateral root shootings can be used as a measure of the increased activity of a growing seedling. This is because in comparison to his control group, there was a great increase in the number of lateral roots that appeared. This effect can be seen in the following photograph:

---
[154](Takamura, 2006)

Chapter 10: The Effects of Electroculture on Plants

Effect of Electrical Stimulation on (Pepper) Plant Roots

Source: plantricity.com[155]

In addition to the above characteristics of roots, they are also responsible for seeking out sources of water. Having a large root system is thus beneficial not only for its ability to draw in nutrients in greater amounts, but also in its ability to locate multiple water sources. Since electroculture often results in plants developing a denser root structure, they then have the ability to transpire greater amounts of water, helping with a number of other functions including the support of photosynthetic function, mineral transport to higher regions, and cooling via evaporation[156].

---
[155] The "Plantricity" system was developed by David MacZura and was at one time published on the website, BroadrOOt.com. The site is now out of service. A blog post about the plantricity system is available on ElectricFertilizer.com.

[156] (Brady, 2012)

Nutrient Uptake Rate

With root hairs being the business end of the root system, their collectively-large surface area is of enormous value with regards to enabling plants to take in great amounts of water and nutrients from the surrounding soil. Root growth in general can profoundly affect this. Since electroculture can help plants with the accelerated production of new lateral roots[157], it can have a significant effect on helping them maximize water and nutrient consumption.

Adjusting the soil conditions can also aid in greater nutrient uptake, allowing for optimal root growth. When roots can easily elongate and spread throughout the ground, this greatly increases their chances of finding a good source of food and water. This occurs most in loose soils with large soil aggregates because the large soil particles provide lots of room for roots to move. It also provides lots of pore space for water and air. As stated before, even if soils are somewhat compacted, the effect of electricity on soil microbes help with creating additional pore space within the soil.

Another process that positively affects nutrient uptake is through the action of ion pumps. When electrically stimulated, increases in metabolic activity cause more frequent ion pumping. The result is an increase in the number of emitted hydrogen ions as a by-product of the transport process. Simultaneously, this would result in an increase in the nutrient uptake rate.

Remember that it's not only the external fields that cause the cellular "doorways" to open up, but also internal changes to the cell's chemistry, too. The net effect is a positive-feedback loop that allows the metabolism to sustain faster operation because the root cells then allow greater amounts of nutrient ions to enter. Combining the effects of an increased root growth along with an increase in the uptake rate subsequently results in a larger amount of nutrient flow than either case individually.

---
[157](Takamura, 2006; ref: Toko and Yamafuji 1988; Ezaki et al. 1990b)

Another aspect that adds to the system is the effect of hydrogen ion increases upon the rhizosphere. Since releases of hydrogen ions directly affect the pH of the surrounding soil, as covered earlier, it will (up to a point) improve the availability of ionic nutrients that happen to be present.

Lastly, recall that the nutrient assimilation rate is also affected not only by the plant's cellular metabolism, but also by the higher metabolic cycles of soil bacteria. Since soil bacteria is needed to convert gaseous nitrogen to a form that plants can use, e.g. nitrates, an increase in bacterial metabolism will cause greater amounts of nitrogen to be converted into a form usable by plants. As long as greater amounts of it are being converted and assimilated, less of it will be released into the atmosphere through denitrification.

Water Intake

The amount of water absorbed by the plant is also affected by the presence of electric fields. In the process of transpiration, water moves up the plant from its roots to its leaves in synchrony with the plant's respiration rate via turgor (water) pressure. When the plant's respiration rate increases, it causes a greater need for water and nutrients from the soil. One can think of this as causing additional amounts of suction upon the root structure, forcing more water into the plant. While this will initially force great amounts of water through the plant's existing root structure, over time, through the effects described above, it will be easier for water to enter the plant because of its electrically-expanded root structure.

Therefore, in the presence of electric fields, it is to be expected that a greater than normal water usage will be needed.

But what if you're growing under conditions where water resources are more scarce? Other physiological changes and an improved response to water stress will help. Read on....

Improved Water Retention

In contrast to an increase in respiration and transpiration under normal growing conditions, depending upon the particulars of each plant's genetics and physiological makeup, it's possible that a plant will respond differently under osmotic stress, i.e. stress from water-scarcity. In the following paragraphs we'll cover modern research that suggests that plants grown under the influence of electric fields can change their innate cellular characteristics, adapting on-the-fly to better handle dry or drought-like conditions.

Normally, cell walls freely let water-soluble substances in and out. Yet under electro-stimulation, the portions of the cell that are normally open can then be closed, helping to prevent any evaporative losses from occurring. This can be a huge benefit for the many growers who experience regular periods of drought!

Let's look at how this may work. We previously covered how cellular calcium levels have a role in the regulation of membrane permeability. When calcium levels are lacking on a cellular level, a phenomenon called ion leakage tends to occur, causing cells and tissues to release significant amounts of water-based molecules and other metabolites.

On the other hand, when an abundance of calcium is present, as shown to be the case when cells and tissues are exposed to electric fields (and assuming that enough calcium is present in the surrounding extracellular fluid), the structure of the cellular membrane tends to be upheld, keeping its innards intact. There's more to it, though. As we covered earlier, high levels of calcium are part of a positive-feedback effect due to its inter-relationship with action potentials. This increase in activity causes greater amounts of hormonal changes to occur, specifically, the synthesis of auxins. Besides being the first plant hormone that was ever discovered, auxins are known for their effects upon cell walls. Having the ability to increase the plasticity or flexibility of cell walls allows for greater amounts of water to be absorbed and held tightly within the cells [158]. So despite the normally increased rate of respiration, water that's already present within the plant's cells will be well-contained, and will not readily exit the plant[159].

Taking this little nugget of knowledge into the realm of real-life field applications, it has been shown in a 2009 study[^FootDrought1] that electricity has positive benefits regarding the drought resistance of seeds. In the study, buckwheat seeds placed under a static electric field experienced an increase in enzymatic activity, which has been known to protect cells against osmotic stress. [^FootDrought1]: (Hua,JunLin,2009) and Paper on Electrical Drought Resistance of Carageenan and (Weisheng, 1999)

Electro-horticultural methods can thus be used to help plants better tolerate droughts. For example, on a divided field of French beans under identical conditions except for electrification, the electrified plot was found to have substantially resisted the dry weather! Regular, uniform growth was observed, resulting in a 300 percent gain in yield compared to the control plot whose beanstalks became completely yellow[160].

In another example[161], electrified passion fruit vines were found to do twice as well compared to ones that weren't electrified, even when grown under near-drought conditions. On top of the increase in yield that was realized, the fruit tended to be larger as well. If water leaked out, as it would under normal conditions, fruit drop or shriveling would have occurred.

Lastly, it's worth noting a secondary reason why electro-horticulture may help plants better survive droughts - via the way that nutrients are transported underground. Under normal conditions, rainwater acts to help decompose more complex organic materials

---

[158](McGrawHill, Chapter 41)
[159](Hepler, 2005)
[160](Christofleau, p.27)
[161](Christofleau, p.29,45+)

found in soils. Yet via in-situ electrolysis reactions, complex nutrients can still be broken down into more usable forms.

Furthermore, these nutrients, both simple and complex, can be easily transported underground using electrokinetic transport. In this way, nutrients beneath the soil can be moved by the influence of the applied electric field, helping plants in dry soils receive the nutrients they need[162] despite a lack of water being available to help with nutrient transport.

Based on these studies, electro-horticulture has gained a whole new application! If crops can be grown in a way such that they can avoid the problems of drought, then in this time of global climate change, this method of growing can be of enormous value to farmers worldwide.

Photosynthesis

Photosynthesis, the mechanism that gives plants the ability to convert light into sugars and other compounds necessary for the creation of energy, is another process that deserves attention. One of the most readily observable results that can be seen after just a few weeks of stimulation is the greening of leaves. Many experimenters have shown how electrically-stimulated plants develop leaves that are thick, lush and dark green.

Diving in, a number of studies suggest that the activation of different hormones may affect the chlorophyll content of leaves as well as their pigmentation. Depending upon the environmental stimulus acting upon the plant, it is known that certain pigments present in chloroplasts may become active in such a way that they can cause the synthesis of additional quantities of themselves resulting in the absorption of greater amounts of light. Since an increase in the cellular respiration rate increases the amount of available carbon dioxide, when combined with an increase in light

---

[162](Christofleau, p.25)

absorption, this has the net effect of increased sugar formation. This eventually results in an increase in ATP.

According to Goldsworthy[163], because calcium acts as the "master volume control" that regulates many aspects of a plant's metabolism, he posited that calcium inflow can also have an effect on chlorophyll synthesis. Under these circumstances, because the plant's metabolism has moved to a "higher gear", it makes sense that the energy generation of the plant would adapt to the changing environmental conditions to make sure that enough food/energy is being produced.

Flowering

A lesser-known fact is that electrical stimuli can affect flowering activities in plants. For instance, in the case studies mentioned in the book Electroculture by Justin Christofleau[164], it was observed that under electrostimulation, the number and size of flower blooms were increased, their perfume was more pronounced, and of course, their foliage was much greener. More than 80 years later, researchers have validated many of these findings, e.g. determining that yield increases[165] are due to improved flowering.

Since plant genetics and enzymatic regulation are also affected, the "Spring switch" that enables springtime flowering[166] can possibly be manipulated to occur earlier in the season when under electrical stimulation. This may yet be another reason for the reports of accelerated growth and earlier harvests.

---

[163] (Goldsworthy, 2006)
[164] (Christofleau, p.45)
[165] (Aladjadjiyan 2002, Alex and Doid, et al., 1995)
[166] Article: The Spring Switch

Summary

Gaining a basic understanding of the fundamentals of soil science, electrochemistry and plant physiology, has given us a more thorough understanding of how the application of electric fields on soils and plants can bring about changes of enormous benefit! These changes are real, and understanding the mechanisms and processes involved will not only help with understanding what's going on, but will also help the reader who is in the role of grower, researcher and inventor as well.

Since plants can grow and adapt to changing physiological and environmental conditions via genetic learning, it may even be possible for plants to be trained to perform better using electricity, and then their offspring may naturally perform better all by themselves. This can be very helpful in research where strains bred for specific purposes can be tested faster, and through electrical stimulation, the expression of certain genes can occur in a more natural fashion, without moving into the realm of direct genetic manipulation.

In the next chapter we'll move on to summarize the positive benefits and applications that can be realized through electroculture.

Chapter 11: Benefits and Applications

"The ears of the crop will be larger and fuller, the leaves of vegetables, fruit trees, vines, and other vegetation will begin to be thicker, larger, greener, the fruit will be larger and more numerous, the vegetables, such as potatoes, tomatoes, beans, etc., will be much larger and more abundant." [*Electroculture* by Justin Christofleau]

Now that we have a basis for the scientific fundamentals of electroculture, we can take a more detailed look at the many benefits that can be realized.

Electro-Tropism

While you have probably heard of the term photo-tropism (the movement of plant limbs towards light) from high-school science class, you may not have learned that plants respond in a similar way in the presence of an electric field. Plants are known to respond directionally to various environmental factors through greater elongations of one set of cells over another set of cells. These are called tropisms. So phototropism is a biological trait that enables plants to maximize exposure to sunlight.

Similarly, with respect to this body of work, there is electrotropism - which is the response of plants to electric fields. As we covered earlier, plants thrive under different types and strengths of electric fields, so it makes sense that the way they behave in response to electricity would be similar to the way they respond to the presence of energy-laden light sources.

The way plants respond to electric fields in an electrotropic manner is by moving their roots towards the positive electrode. How could this be useful? One idea is that if it is found that a certain type of grass seed responds well to electroculture, then it could possibly be used to help spread the root system over a wider area, rather than just deeper. This could help with erosion to some degree. Perhaps it could be used as a way of eliminating bare-spots in the soil - by letting plant roots spread to places where they would normally not grow.

Growth Rate

One of the commonly observed traits is that plants are seen to grow at an accelerated rate. This opens up a number of implications that can be very valuable to the small-scale or commercial grower. For instance, if crops can be grown in a faster manner such that their crop can be harvested earlier than normal, the following benefits may be able to be realized:

- **Reducing Risk of Frost-Damage**: When a risk of frost damage exists due to a late harvest, the risk can be lessened by harvesting weeks earlier.
- **Improving Short Grow-Season Seed Constraints**: Instead of planting seed varieties that have shorter growing seasons, the grower may be able to plant seeds with longer maturation times to differentiate themselves from the other regional growers.
- **Improving Intensive Crops**: Intensive gardeners who aim to stagger the growth of multiple crops in a season may be able squeeze out an extra growth cycle to further increase crop productivity.

- **Improving Profitability**: There can be significant financial gains due to the early harvest of commodity crops because prices are typically at their peak at the very beginning of the harvest period, when supplies are often at their lowest. It may be possible to multiply one's earnings with an early delivery to the market.

These last points can also be used in indoor or urban growing scenarios, where only small amounts of grow-space are available. By maximizing the efficiency of your grow-space, perhaps multiple (or even multiplied) yields could be realized.

This can be seen in many real life experiments. In addition to the cases in Chapter 3, the author/experimenter Justin Christofleau[167] wrote about a crop of melons and cucumbers that germinated in 4 to 5 days compared to the rest of his crop that sprouted more than 10 days later. A 2-week or 10-day lead could be invaluable! I have observed this in my own experiments on Romanesco broccoli and other vegetables where, within one and a half months, the electrified plant group was approximately twice as tall as the normal plant group. If these types of gains are possible in the very beginning of the plant's growth period, then it makes sense that over the course of the plant's life, cumulative reductions in growth time could be possible.

Enhanced Fruit Ripening

The acceleration effect can also be seen in the ripening process as well. Through a quickening of enzymatic processes and the early synthesis of ripening hormones like ethylene, it was discovered that fruits could actually ripen faster when placed under electrical stimulation[168]. Combining the effects of accelerating crop growth with a faster ripening process, growers using these techniques can

---
[167](Christofleau, p.59)
[168](Jain: Boe and Salunkhe 1963)

realize enormous gains resulting in an increase in profits as well as a huge reduction of weather-related risks as well.

Accelerated Tree Growth

In the 1930s, Dr. Marinesco (mentioned earlier in Chapter 9), found that the application of an electric field to a bundle of capillary tubes submerged in an electrically-conductive solution resulted in the movement of liquid through all of the tubes. In essence, he found a way of demonstrating the concept of electro-osmosis using thin tubes instead of using lots of small particles like sand or soil. He later postulated that if an electric field were to be applied to a tree (with its own set of bundled vascular channels, the xylem and phloem), there may be a similar movement of fluid.

It turned out that his theory was correct. Applying an[169] electric field between the plant roots and a point higher up in the tree caused an increase in the movement of sap.

Based on the results of similar experiments, if the positive terminal were placed high above the ground, and the negative one placed into the ground, this could help draw sap into the upper reaches of the tree, further assisting the plant in delivering nutrients from the roots to other parts of the tree, against the force of gravity. Using this technique may not only improve the movement of sap, but also its production.

While electrically manipulating the flow of sap in trees is possible, what benefits, if any, does it really bring to trees? Consider the following examples of what can be done:

- Trees experience vigorous, faster growth
- Larger and sweeter fruit is produced
- Increases number of shooting branches, improving yield

---

[169](Seifriz, 1929) and (Dorchester, 1937; p9)

Chapter 11: Benefits and Applications   133

- Increases fruit ripening by two weeks or more[170][171]
- Faster resin production
- Reduction or slowing down of the plant's aging process[172]
- Radically improves the health of sick trees
- Potentially protects trees against frost
- Improves pollination[173]
- Improves the cleaning of air from toxic pollutants[174]

Christofleau was a prominent inventor, scientist and author from the early-mid 1900s. He describes a number of case studies in his book (mentioned above) that exemplify the successes that people have had with electroculture on trees. One client had an old pear tree that was so old and frail that most of its bark had fallen off its trunk and it barely had any leaves on it. Upon applying electricity to it, its heath turned around and it started producing a large number of pears weighing up to one pound, each[175].

In a similar situation was an apricot tree that had a fungal infection. After electrical treatment, it took on a whole new look with intensely green vegetation, new and healthy shoots, and the complete disappearance of the fungus. Other tree ailments that have been known to have been healed include curl leaf in peach and nectarine trees[176].

I have seen a similar state of recovery in my own experiments. One was a small fig shoot that was taking a very long time to develop its initial leaves. While waiting for it to start growing, my pet parrot got loose one day and tore an inch-long gash in the tiny stalk (about 1/4 inch in diameter). Amazingly, after applying electricity to the

---

[170](Christofleau, 1927 p16), (Truffault, 1935)
[171]*Cyclopedia of American Agriculture*, 1911
[172](Goldsworthy, 2006; ref: Selaga & Selaga 1996)
[173]According to master gardener Steve Brady, when there is an increase in the airflow within the inside of peach trees, helping with pollination via Steve Brady on "The Master Gardener Hour", 5/19/12.
[174]"TreeHugger.com Article on How tree leaves capture particulate matter pollution
[175](Christofleau, 1927 p24)
[176](Christofleau, 1927 p49)

plant for a few weeks, leaves started to appear despite the heavy damage. On the other hand, as a testament to the fact that this technology is not a cure-all, is that I applied 12 volts to out borer-infested pear tree at home and found that it didn't do a thing.

It is worth noting that if the polarity is reversed between trunk and roots, that growth may be stunted. Why is this worth mentioning? Because for some types of growth, e.g. bonsai, dwarfism is desired. Other benefits may come from the dwarfing of trees that are situated too close to your home.

Improved Fruits and Vegetables Size

What's amazing about electroculture is the vast number of experiments that demonstrate significant increases in the size of fruits and vegetables. Consider the following:

- Christofleau had carrots that grew to 19 inches and beets to almost 6 inches in diameter. He found similar results with tomatoes, French beans, asparagus, artichokes and celery.
- In the 1850s, The Cyclopedia of American Agriculture described an experimenter named Ross who grew an electrified crop of potatoes that ended up being five times larger than his unelectrified crop.
- Around the same time, Russian researcher Speschnew grew radishes 17 inches long and 5 inches in diameter. He also claimed to be able to grow a carrot 11 inches in diameter and weighing almost five pounds[177].

In a 2006 study entitled "Influence of electric field on plant weight[178]", it was proposed that hormones like gibberellins may be the reason for the increase in size. The size and weight increased; yet after the

---
[177](Hull, 1898)
[178](Shimizu, 2009)

removal of water by vacuum treatment, the sample weight turned out to be less than the group without treatment. This suggests that water absorption is the primary means by which the growth in increased. Yet keep in mind that this is just one study, on one type of plant. Knowing that different plant species respond differently, it is feasible to suggest that other types may exhibit an increase in plant matter (in addition to "water weight").

For example, in another study, onion plants (*Allium cepa L.*) were shown to increase in weight in both fresh as well as dry seedlings[179]. In this case, it was posited that one of the reasons for weight gain beyond the increase in water weight could be an improved synthesis of sugars[180]. At the same time, increased amounts of cellulose found in the rapidly growing stems and roots could also be a contributing factor.

Crop Yield

One of the most beneficial results that can be achieved through the use of electro-horticulture is the booting of yield. With all factors being equal except for the addition of electrical fields upon the soil or plants themselves, experiencing gains from 30 to 400 percent in certain cases is astounding to say the least.

Returning to the work of Christofleau, in his book on electroculture, he claimed that at during one bad year, he grew some oats in his control plot with stalks that grew to be under three feet tall with an average of 29 grains per ear. In comparison, in his electrified field, the average plant was four feet tall with approximately 54 grains per ear - an 86% gain! In the same time period, other people who grew oats as well as wheat, maize, and millet saw improvements between 75% and 100%[181].

---
[179](Jain,2011; ref (Alexander and Doijode, 1995))
[180]Applied Electrical Phenomena, 1966
[181](Christofleau, 1927 p24,50-59)

Some experimenters that I've been in touch with since starting my research have told me of their own successes with yield as well. For example, tomato growers Weber & Lang experienced to back-to-back seasons with yield increases ranging from 40% to over 50%.

Likewise, a person who planning on implementing a commercial permaculture farm in Peru has told me that preliminary experiments proved that he was able to achieve a xx% yield increase in his grape tomato crop.

The scientific underpinnings behind the increases are two-fold:

- Increased shoot development
- Increased budding
- Earlier flowering While some claim that the differences come from earlier flowering[182], I prefer the research from Christofleau and his clients from the early 1920s who suggested that yield increases in trees may be due to increased shoot production. Takamura and others have found that lateral root formation is improved; this may be a similar effect, except being above-ground. Improvements in shoot development are related to having an increased number of bud sites.

Taste of Fruits and Vegetables

Some historical accounts have made references to electrically-treated fruit and vegetable plants as being not only larger in size, but better tasting, too! A physiological explanation for this effect may be due to gibberellic acid's effect on inducing seedless fruits[^FootSeedless]. When fruits are induced into growing in this manner, they not only demonstrate higher yields, but their sugar content has been known to significantly increase. This would explain the better taste that people have experienced.

---

[182](Jain,2011; ref (Aladjadjiyan 2002, Alex and Doid... 1995))

As an example, it has also been found that the application of electric fields to barley plants results in increases in sugar formation. Additional barley experiments reviewed in the magazine, *Applied Electrical Phenonema*[183] revealed that the greatest effect was on the formation of sucrose compared to the other sugars that were found to be present.

My own thoughts on the matter have to do with how plant leaves become greener than normal. If through the deepening of plant and stem pigmentation occurs, then photosynthetic efficiency increases as well. This will cause the conversion of greater amounts of absorbed light-energy into sugars, used not only for maintaining an increased metabolism (amongst other enhanced physiological processes), but also for putting into additional stores inside fruiting bodies. Perhaps through the careful modulation of the electric field that deliberately sweeter-tasting fruits and vegetables can be developed???

Nutritional Value

Since ion uptake is improved via the accelerated intake of water and nutrients, it follows that the general nutritional value of the plant's fruiting bodies (e.g. fruits, vegetables and nuts) will also be improved. Another reason behind the improvement in nutrition comes from the way that soil ions are made more readily available, both through the electrokinetic transport of nutrients from a wider area around the plant as well as through improvements nutrient conversion efficiency.

---
[183] Applied Electrical Phenonema, 1966

Healing Response to Disease

In addition to benefits that can come about as a result of improved growth and nutrition, electricity can assist in boosting the tissue regeneration and the general self-healing capabilities of plants as well.

While it has been known that electric fields have long been used in promoting healing in people, it seems reasonable that similar effects could be realized on plant tissues as well. In mammals, for instance, one place where electricity is used in healing is in the accelerated healing of bones or skin wounds. After a traumatic bone or spinal injury, doctors have seen great benefit from electrically-stimulated bone regrowth. The same methods have also been applied to skin injuries, where electrodes applied to either side of a gaping wound have been found to not only accelerate the rate of healing, but to reduce the level of pain as well.

With respect to plants, a number of research projects are going on covering the topic of electrotherapy, or the healing of plant-based diseases with electricity. Since the purpose of this book is to focus on the acceleration aspects of plant growth, only a brief listing will be presented.

Plants, like people, have been found to respond very favorably to electrotherapy. This can be both a side-effect of soil-based or direct-to-plant electrostimulation. Below is a list of some of the healing and rejuvenatory effects that can be realized:

- Destruction of parasites
- Prevention of root rot
- Reduction or prevention of frost damage
- Reduction or prevention of mildew and other fungi
- Revival after wilting
- Healing of blight

- Healing of phylloxera in grape vines[184]
- Destruction of superbugs like E. coli[185]
- Prevention or treatment of chlorosis[186]
- Curing of Ratoon stunting disease in sugarcane[187].
- Healing of plants against viruses including: Potato virus Y, Potato leafroll virus[188], Bean common mosaic virus[189], and other viruses of the genus potyvirus[190], luteovirus[191] and carlavirus[192] [193].

The above list is just a sampling of what's likely possible using electricity in the treatment of plant-based afflictions. Some researchers suggest that the increase in action potentials causes a wound-healing response. While further research is needed as to the underlying reasons behind the healing response, this is a promising area that is ripe for exploration.

Summary

The purpose of this chapter has been to show the wide body of benefits that are possible. The number of effects upon the plant physiology itself are staggering: faster metabolism, optimized conversion of light into sugars and energy, accelerated nutrient uptake, hormonal and genetic activations and more. With all of the positive effects that can be achieved through using the methods of electroculture, now is a time that is ripe for gardeners, farmers and experimenters alike to reap the benefits. This knowledge can

---
[184] (Christofleau, 1927 p23-25,29,59)
[185] (Zvitov, Zohar-Perez, Nussinovitch)
[186] A condition in which leaves produce insufficient chlorophyll.
[187] Guillen, Hernandez, Rodriguez, Gomez - 2007
[188] (Dhital, Hak Tae Lim, Sharma)
[189] (Hormozi-Nejad, Mozafari, Rakhshandehroo)
[190] http://en.wikipedia.org/wiki/Potyvirus
[191] http://en.wikipedia.org/wiki/Luteovirus
[192] http://en.wikipedia.org/wiki/Carlavirus
[193] [(Hernandez, J.A. et al., 1995 via Gonzalez)]

be used to not only improve the growth of our crops, but more importantly to help with the creation of a more productive and sustainable food production system. So whether you're an urban gardener trying to grow some salad greens on your balcony or the manager of a large scale farming operation, the benefits are the same, just at different levels of scale.

Now that we're finished explaining the history of electroculture, the science behind the way it works, and the benefits that can be realized, we will move forward and explore some new applications that can be the basis for future experimental work in this area.

Chapter 12: New Application Ideas

Electro-Horticulture follows organic practices, enabling growth-hormone based improvements to occur biologically rather than synthetically.

By taking into account the many physiological changes that occur under stimulation, a number of new applications for electroculture can be realized beyond simple growth acceleration. Below are some application ideas that can provide substantial benefits to growers who are willing to give electro-horticulture a try.

- Improving integrated pest management
- Improving pollination
- Extending cool-climate growing seasons
- Defending crops against drought
- Protecting against early frosts
- Improving grazing management

Integrated Pest Management (IPM)

While there aren't enough studies in this area, several people have noted that electrically-stimulated plants tend to repel insects from harming them[194]. From aphids to mosquitoes[195], and parasites too, electroculture could be a healthy alternative to the use of insecticides when used as a part of an IPM plan. When your crop

---
[194](Takamura,2006)
[195](Ennis,2012)

is under attack, rather than bringing out the chemicals (which is one strategy), perhaps the crop can be put though an electrification cycle. This idea is based on some field notes from a number of growers who found this to be true within their grow-rooms.

The science behind these claims, as explained in one paper, states that aphids can be repelled from strawberries through chemicals released via stimulated gene expression[196]. Some of the other mechanisms are as follows:

- Wounded plants can emit a variety of volatile organic compounds(VOCs) that affect not only the lone plant being attacked, but surrounding plants as well.
- Different sets of genes can be activated based on signal transduction, triggered from the plant's immune system when under attack.
- Emitted VOCs can repel harmful insects while simultaneously attracting predatory insects.
- Interactions with neighboring plants may elicit others to emit complementary compounds to help fend off an attack.

It may have to do with the rate at which a cocktail of volatile aromatic compounds are exuded from the plant's leaves and flowers. Some plants have natural self-defense capabilities against insects or parasites, so under electrical stimulation, these effects may be accentuated. Dr. Eric Davies, professor and head of North Carolina State University's Department of Biology says that during experiments performed on tomato plants, he noted that electrical signals (APs) from injured cells can trigger rapid gene expression that lead to an increase in the production of proteinase inhibitors. Also known as PINs, these chemicals are known for increasing the plant's resistance to insect feeding damage.[197]

---

[196](Dudareva,Pichersky,2006)
[197]See (Henehan, 1997)

Chapter 12: New Application Ideas   143

The mechanisms behind this are multifold. Because of the plant's increased metabolism, these compounds are stimulated into overproduction. Next, based on the increased respiration, greater amounts of compounds can be exhaled into the nearby atmosphere. The effect is further amplified through inter-plant communication messages which may cause nearby plants to exude these substances as well[198], creating a 'crowd-sourced' defense mechanism.

In addition to creating volatile chemicals that may repel certain insects, these compounds have also been used to attract parasitic insects that feed upon attackers[199]. An example of a predator attractant behavior is this: when certain genes in potato plants are activated, they cause the release of chemicals which make them attractive to predatory mites[200].

This process isn't without risks. While plants can emit substances toxic for insect attackers, too much can prove harmful for the plant. Even though the toxic chemicals are generated within the plant, if inhaled, it can cause stress. A negative factor in addition to the risk of self-poisoning is the production cost of these compounds. Since plants typically consume greater amounts of energy when under attack, prolonged chemical generation can adversely affect systems that require great amounts of energy, like reproductive functions, which may affect fruit production. While it may be possible for the stress to be minimized from greater nutrient intake, in the long run it depends on the plant species, the length of time of the attack, the insect's resistance to the counter-attack, and other factors.

Attraction of Pollinators

We now know that plants that thrive under electrical influence not only respire more, but experience an increase the production

---
[198] (Paré,Tumlinson, 1999)
[199] (Moraes, Lewis, Paré, Alborn, Tumlinson), (Paré,Tumlinson, 1999), (Dudareva,Pichersky,2006)
[200] (Dudareva,Pichersky,2006)

of aromatic compounds that are synthesized in response to certain stimuli (e.g. insect attack). We also know that oftentimes plants will become more green in color, in both stems and leaves, indicating an improvement in photosynthesis and subsequently, sugar or energy production.

With these changes going on behind the scenes, pollinating insects may find themselves more attracted to the sweet smell of electrically-charged plants compared to normally grown ones[201]. Furthermore, since respiration is also increased, plants can be expected to thus "exhale" more of its perfume into the atmosphere, drawing in more bees, wasps, and other pollinating species. If this can be field-verified, then the use electroculture can create significant benefits to farmers who need pollination services.

Taking this a step further would be using electroculture to attract bees and other desired insects to a particular crop of interest. By having a field grown in this manner with your own colonies of bees serving it, you can encourage them to take in pollen and nectar from the healthier form of electrically-stimulated plants. For organic farmers and honey producers, this can be a way of helping to keep honey bees close to home, with the goal of producing an especially aromatic perfume that may be helpful for keeping your bees away from other properties where chemical or genetically-treated crops may be grown.

This will result in not only healthier bees that will be less susceptible to pathogens, but also end-products that will be better for the health and well-being of the consumer. Imagine being able to create the conditions for a healthier set of bee-related products ranging from honey, to pollen, and even beeswax.

Another application would be using electricity-stimulated crops to steer bees towards a particularly desired crop, especially when multiple nectar-producing varieties are in season at the same time. For instance, if you have a crop of lavender and you want honey

---

[201](Dudareva,Pichersky, 2006)

that's primarily composed of lavender-based nectar, then you can turn that crop on and direct most of your bees to that crop. A side benefit for the electro-apiarist (A new term), would be the benefit of attracting other bees in the area to your crop with a magnified scent of nectar. Assuming that you're following natural beekeeping practices, it may also be a best practice for the native bees.

Season Extension, Frost and Drought Protection

In addition to being beneficial for attracting desired insects and repelling undesired ones, electroculture can be used to help cold-climate growers as well. For example, the acceleration effect that comes from crops grown with electrical stimulation can be used for not only reducing risk from weather-related crop losses, but also with increasing the commodity crop ROI with better market timing. In this section we'll explore some of these possible applications.

Rapid Food Growth in Survival, Disaster Response, and Quarantine Situations

For people experiencing nature's random upheavals upon life, like being placed into various forms of survival situations, electroculture can provide great benefit through the production of greater amounts of food, or the harvest of food sooner than normal. When applied to fast-growing crops, such as sprouting environments (e.g. mung, alfalfa, etc.) - electroculture can potentially speed up the harvest cycle by a few days. To improve things even further, a number of electroculture sprout systems can be used simultaneously to improve harvests over the long-term, providing a healthy form of sustenance for a long time using minimal space for the storage of beans, etc.

Of course, for those with enough area for a proper grow environment indoors or outdoors, electroculture's benefits to normal fruit and vegetable plants can be applicable as well.

Cool Climate Farming

For growers in cooler climates, whether it's in the deep northern or southern hemispheres, or at higher elevations, farmers can realize an earlier harvest due to the growth acceleration effect. An early harvest can not only be beneficial from a market standpoint, where the grower may be able to supply the market while prices are high (before most growers are able to deliver to market), but also from a risk-management standpoint.

Due to the changing and volatile environmental conditions going on worldwide, more and more people in many parts of the world may have to deal with earlier frost dates, which can kill off a crop overnight with the onset of a sudden freeze. Electroculture may provide a way to mitigate this risk.

It could do so in the following ways:

- Rapid growth allows for earlier harvesting
- Expression of latent cold-hardy genetics hidden within the crops' DNA.
- Stimulating the crop into operating at a higher rate, much akin to the ways some animals stay warm in the winter by having a higher metabolic rate. This could help the plant to stay alive during deep freezes.

Frost Protection

Currently, in order to protect plants from frost, it must be done with a small to medium scale using cold frames or cloches, or at a larger scale by using a heated greenhouse. A third possibility exists that can help with extending the season of plants not only within the cold frames, but also those that are situated in the open air.

While few have studied the effects of electroculture on frost protection, experimenters such as Justin Christofleau claimed that tomato plants and other crops could be protected against damage from light freezes [202]. Despite the minimal number of case studies that can be found, I propose that the effects are well substantiated by a scientific understanding of the principles described in the preceding chapters.

As previously described, the flow of sap can be manipulated through electrical stimulation. This suggests that as long as the sap is still in a liquid state, that freezing at moderately cold temperatures could be thwarted. Aside from the movement of sap, remember that due to the propagation of action potentials and calcium-mediated chemical signals the entire plant operates at a much higher metabolic rate. This increase could help the plant with compensating against the slowing effect that cold weather has on the rate of intra-cellular fluid flow and the slowing of biochemical reactions.

Technically, many plants have inbred genetic traits that help with surviving freezing temperatures. Mechanisms include processes that can bring about changes to cellular structure, stabilizing cell membranes against freeze-induced injury[203]. Similar to the way cell membranes can become more flexible so they can stretch and grow larger while holding greater amounts of water, the same holds true the other way, with genes that may be available for helping bolster cell walls against breakage under cold-stress. Furthermore, the basics still apply: faster metabolic activity helps with compensating against the cold weather slowing of plants' biochemical reactions[204].

---
[202](Christofleau, Justin, 2007: p25,48)
[203](Thomashow,Michael, 1999)
[204](Goss)

From a commercial grower point of view, since trees and row crops can experience not only accelerated growth of their limbs, leaves, flowers and fruit, in combination with accelerated ripening times and engineered resistance against early frosts, major financial benefits that may be attained.

Drought Protection

For those who live in arid climates, or even temperate environments that experience large shifts in their water cycle, drought can be a major problem! Without (much) rainwater or supplemental irrigation, many plants can die from deep osmotic stress. Under dehydration, the following lists the physiological changes that can ensue:

- Accumulation of solutes[205], leading to harmful increases in concentration.
- Reduction in photosynthesis
- Cell shrinkage

While a number of promising improvements for drought management, including the use of drought-resistant GMO crops and the use of drip-irrigation methods, consider the benefits that electrically-stimulated farmland can bring. If you can recall, there are a number of physiological changes that can take place in plants, described in Chapter 10. In summary, there can be a significant reduction in water losses due to:

- Increased strength of cell walls
- Increased flexibility of cell walls
- Reduced ion leakage effects
- Expression of genetic traits that combat osmotic-stress

---

[205]Particles dissolved within a liquid solution.

- Enzymatic changes affecting transpiration
- Better ability to grow deeper roots

As such, electroculture can be a huge help for crops growing under low-water drought conditions, helping millions, even under adverse and rapidly changing environmental conditions.

Accelerated Cleanup of Contaminated Soils

While dealing with adverse weather conditions is a place where electroculture hold enormous benefit, a lesser-known area that's also important, especially regarding the long-term effects of growing food outside, is dealing with growing land contaminated with toxic chemicals.

What land is considered contaminated? Certainly there are "brownfield" sites that look like toxic wastelands... But I'm not growing food there. Are you sure this topic is relevant to me, the average grower?

Absolutely... Let me tell you how. In my own case, I first became interested in this topic after moving into a new house with my wife a bunch of years ago. While clearing away a huge swath of ground in the back yard with the intention of creating a food garden, underneath the years of neglect and the piles of vines and weeds I found all sorts of interesting modern artifacts. I found old car parts and pieces of motors, lots of broken glass and old pieces of wiring and piping.

While I didn't know what the use of this piece of land was 50 or more years ago, I do know that seeing this stuff in the soil made me feel a little nervous. Ultimately it became the cause of my piqued interest in a topic called remediation, or the science of cleaning soil from modern pollutants.

Chapter 12: New Application Ideas   150

So, what is someone who comes across this particular problem supposed to do? The approach that government agencies take is to typically remove all of the contaminated dirt to a certain depth earth using earth movers and dump trucks. The soil is then replaced with clean dirt sometime in the future. Other methods are available too, ranging from the use of chemicals, electricity[206], and even bacteria that consumes chemical hydrocarbons as food.

But for the average land-owner, there's a relatively low-cost solution that's also available... phytoremediation!

Phytoremediation is a process that employs certain plants to help with cleaning the soil of certain toxic contaminants. It turns out that some plants that are especially well suited for the task. These are called "hyperaccumulators". Wikipedia[207] has a good list of plants that you can check out. For example, sunflowers[208] are known for the removal of lead and radioactive substances. In fact, they have been used for the removal of radioactive cesium from Fukushima, Japan.

However, the process of phytoremediation is very time consuming - it simply takes a long time for the plants to grow. But what if we want to accelerate the process?

Using electroculture, we can accelerate the cleanup via the following mechanisms:

- Growing faster, pulling in greater amounts of contaminated compounds into its tissues.
- Growing larger in size, larger stems, leaves and even fruits will hold more.
- Electromigration effects in the soil will allow for the root systems to receive more contaminants from a larger area.

---

[206] Via various forms of electrokinetic remediation... using electricity to direct contaminants towards special 'vacuum-like' electrodes that suck up contaminants based on their electrical polarity.
[207] http://en.wikipedia.org/wiki/List_of_hyperaccumulators
[208] http://www.japantoday.com/category/national/view/sunflowers-used-to-clean-up-radiation

I have been involved with a project called the Sunflower+ Project StL[209] that took on the task of improving the look of urban wastelands by growing a field of sunflower plants. Assuming that the land would be lead contaminated, for the first few years the sunflowers would be used for removing heavy-metal contaminants. Later, once deemed safe for growing food crops on, the sunflowers would continue to grow with the purpose of helping urban youth with the creation of a business venture related to the plot, e.g. processing the seeds into nut butters.

In my time experimenting on sunflowers, I learned that they could be stimulated successfully into growing taller than control-group plants with as little as 1.5 volts, depending upon the species. I also learned that the results are species-dependent - so the response between two or more types of sunflower seeds may vary. This was expected. Anyhow, while there could have certainly been confounding variables present in this outdoor experiment, generally we found the electrified plants to grow more than 8 inches taller than the control group, on average. Unfortunately (as well as fortunately, too), the initial soil-lead tests that were performed revealed that the plot had very low levels present, well within the acceptable range for being deemed "safe". I say it's unfortunate because it would have been very interesting to learn how much lead could have been retrieved from an electrified plant compared to a regular one.

It's also worth noting that in addition to using plants for remediation, beneficial microorganisms can be used as well. While plants tend to be best for removing heavy metals out of the ground, certain microbial families excel at neutralizing various chemical compounds often found in waste products. This process, called bioremediation or bioaugmentation, can also be improved using electricity through making them more active than usual. To learn more about this check out our Resources[210] page.

---

[209]https://www.facebook.com/SunflowerProjectstl
[210]http://ElectricFertilizer.com/book-resources/

Summary

The purpose of this chapter has been to show off what's possible by those growing plants or trees using electricity. The number of effects upon the physiology of plants lends itself to finding numerous applications for it. From improving healing response and its use in disease control, to its ability to make the cell walls take on a denser form for the purpose of drought control, many areas can be improved upon.

Even though our understanding of the total set of effects is vastly incomplete, the current body of knowledge regarding electroculture's effects can be hugely beneficial for gardeners, farmers and experimenters alike. The applications of these technologies can have an enormous effect on improving lives and profits. Profit and loss can be better managed in both cool as well as hot weather regions

In addition to maximizing yields or mitigating losses, it can be used for creative applications in other forms of agribusiness too, such as in apiary management, animal husbandry, agroforestry, and more. Electro-horticulture is a centuries-old technology that needs to be resurrected once again so the benefits of its use can spread. Not only can it provide enormous functional benefits, but once the initial system is installed, its maintenance cost is negligible since the energy needs of these systems are extremely low.

In the next chapter we'll show you how to easily build your own system using parts found in your home. We'll also share with you some ideas for experimentation that you can try. So, please, read on, build your own system, and join the ranks of researchers and experimenters who have also achieved great results from soil and plant electrification.

Chapter 13: Try It Yourself!

Electrically-stimulated agriculture can be applied in a wide number of horticultural environments ranging from small-scale potted plants to large-scale greenhouses. With the right design, it can even be used in outdoor farming situations. Creating your own systems to experiment with is easy. At a minimum, a system can be built using commonly available components found within most households. In this chapter we will cover everything you need to know for constructing a system of your own. Here is a brief summary of the steps you need to follow:

1. Collect system components
2. Prepare power supply for use
3. Attach wires to electrodes
4. Insert into growing medium
5. Power on and observe!

Let's get into the details and start by listing the components of these systems.

What You'll Need

To put a system together you'll need the following:

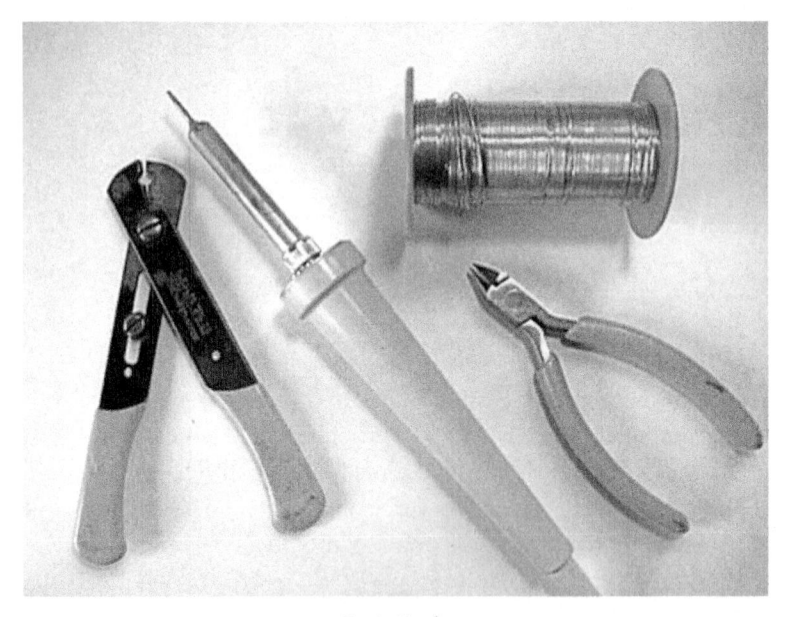

Basic Tools

Source: http://www.mignonette-game.com/assembly.php

- Some basic tools like wire strippers, pliers. Optional: A soldering iron with solder and flux.
- A power source like a wall charger or battery
- Hook-up wire
- Electrodes: iron or steel nails
- A growing container complete with soil and seed

Tools

While you can probably get by using a pocket knife or scissors, it would be much easier to use tools specifically made for working with wires, like a pair of wire strippers/cutters.

If you want to make your system more robust, having a decent soldering iron would be best as it would help to ensure that the electrical connections are both electrically and mechanically sound.

To verify that the system is put together correctly, you should use an electrical testing tool like a digital voltmeter that can measure voltage, current and resistance. It should also be able to check for circuit continuity.

To learn more about these tools, check out our resources[211].

Power Source

When external electric fields are applied to plants, their cells respond in a number of ways. These fields can be applied in a myriad of ways including:

- Application of direct-current (DC) power to the soil or to parts of the plant itself
- Application of time-varying voltage waveforms, e.g. AC (alternating current) power or pulsed DC waveforms
- High voltage static or time-varying electric fields through the soil or air

While there may be some differences in the plants' physiological responses based on the method of stimulation, the results will be similar to that of the DC stimulation approach, which is the focus of this book.

---
[211] http://electrocfertilizer.com/book-resources

> 🔑 **Optimal Power Levels** Best voltages for green stem plants are 1V, 3V and 5V. Best currents are 5 microAmps to 0.55 mA.[212]
>
> Note that different types of plants may respond negatively to a voltage that's too high. So, when possible, try to keep the voltages you use at 5 volts or less. Exceptions: Some experimenters have found that approximately 30 volts is sufficient for direct-tree stimulation, but for most in-soil electroculture, this may be too way much overkill. Of course this all depends on soil type, conductivity, moisture levels, and the distance between the electrodes. Likewise, they may also respond negatively to too much electrical current. If this is the case (as determined by experimentation), a current-limiting resistor can be added into the stimulation circuit between the battery and one of the electrodes, or alternatively, the current density could be decreased through the use of a larger electrode. See the electrode section for more details.

To electrify the soil, a source of power is needed. Depending upon your need, power can be obtained from one or a combination of the following power sources:

- Dedicated line-powered power supplies
- Batteries
- Power generation equipment, e.g. solar panels

Line-Powered Power Supplies

---
[212](Cyclopedia)

Chapter 13: Try It Yourself! 157

An Assortment of Wall Chargers

Source: HowToGeek.com[213]

While this source of power can come from many different places, the easiest and most readily available source for most people is a battery charger that you may have laying about from an old cellphone or other consumer electronics device. These types of power supplies have a typical power rating of 3 to 5 volts (VDC) at approximately 250 milliamps (mA) being equal to about 1.25 watts of power. If the power supply you have operates under different specifications, that's okay too. In practice, far-less than the rated current will be used in your plants.

> Note: Some power supplies label the cord in such a way that the positive lead is marked, e.g. with a white stripe. At this time the polarity of the power supply does not matter.

Battery-based Power Supplies

Batteries can be a great way of setting up a remotely-powered system for very little cost. Even if the batteries need to be replaced

---

[213] http://www.howtogeek.com/93346/undertanding-wall-wart-power-supplies-electronics/

from time to time, while it is a big inconvenience, for those who are in cost-sensitive situations, it can be a good option for getting started.

Yet batteries have a number of drawbacks, as to be described in the following paragraphs.

The first problem is that batteries need to be sized correctly. If the battery gets "loaded" too much, or it's presented with too much of a current draw, then its lifetime can be severely affected. For example, when the soil is medium-dry, it could be considered to be a normal condition. Yet when the soil is wet, or soaking-wet, the current flow will be much higher because when more water is present, the soil resistance will be much lower than normal, allowing for greater amounts of current to flow. In addition to altering the battery's life, it will cause the voltage to "sag", or lower it's voltage. If it sags too much, then the amount of power present in the soil may not be high enough to cause a plant to physiologically react.

To compensate for this, a stiffer power source would need to be used. What this means is that the battery would need to have a higher power capacity. With higher capacity comes the ability to handle higher current draws, if needed. More than one hundred years ago, experimenters were able to get by with only 1.5 volts or less by using large plates that effectively acted like a large, stiff power supply, providing a means for the current to flow over large distances without dropping the voltage much. These were equivalent to using multiple single-cell batteries in parallel, giving them the ability to have much more power on hand, negating the voltage droop problems that occur when low-powered batteries are put under too much of an electrical load. Today, this would be accomplished using larger-sized batteries, or a number of smaller ones connected in series via a battery holder. Large-sized batteries that may suffice could range from a lawnmower battery to a few 'D' cell batteries connected together in series, as they are used in large handheld flashlights.

Unless there is extra circuitry present to alert the user that the voltage is too low, over long-periods of time, you will not know whether the system is working correctly. To get around this you could consider using a multimeter to simply test your battery to see where its power levels are. This approach would need to be repeated every so often and would be a hassle. If the voltage ends up being too low, then the battery would need to be replaced or recharged. At the same time though, since only very minute amounts of power are needed to cause a physiological effect (micro-Amps to milli-Amps), a decline in battery voltage may not be detrimental in electroculture systems as compared to normal electronic devices. In fact, I would argue that small-scale electroculture experiments could be a great way of utilizing the last bits of charge that are present in 'dead' batteries.

Power Generation Equipment

Lastly, with the cost of solar cells falling and the emergence of new forms of power generation, it's worth sharing the benefits of using power-generating equipment, especially for remote operation. In the past decade or so, a number of tried and true, as well as novel power-generation systems have become available. By using these systems in your remote electro-horticulture applications, you can be assured of year-round success with little need for worrying about the power system failing. Let's discuss some of the possibilities:

- Solar power
- Wind or water power
- Microbial power

Solar power is the most readily available power generation equipment that can be found today. Solar cells are relatively inexpensive and the technological know-how for creating robust generation equipment is widely available. In solar power, a solar cell, or many cells (called a solar array or panel) are wired up in a series or in parallel to generate the power that's needed.

Wind or water can also be used via generator equipment. While higher in cost than solar equipment, in places where solar cells may have limited availability, wind or water mills that generate electricity can be used to power a patch of land. With a generator-based power system, the amount of voltage and current produced is dependent upon the speed of rotation. These systems require greater amounts of circuit knowledge because the batteries they charge (or in the fields they power directly) will need to be protected against over-voltage, which can cause damage to batteries and crops.

In both solar- and wind-powered generation systems, the amount of power available for generation is proportional to the availability of the sun and the wind, respectively. For 24-hour operation where the generator is effectively charging a battery, the power system would need to be designed to have enough generation capacity to keep the battery at a place where 90 percent of its voltage is available for electroculture (assuming the batteries are 1.5 volts). Most generation systems output between 5 and 24 volts, so additional circuitry would be needed to step down the voltage as needed.

The last generation technology I'm going to cover is microbial power through the use of microbial fuel cells, also known as MFCs. These work similarly to electroculture systems in that certain electrodes are placed into a medium containing lots of microbes, e.g. sewer water, dirt, and other microbial-rich substances. The electrodes will pick up power that's released from the bacteria, and the wires to which they are attached can be used to power a wide number of low-power devices.

While the power output from these devices is low, multiple MFCs can be used together to increase the available power. The benefit of using this type of device over solar and wind is that they operate continually, day and night, meaning that battery power would not be needed.

Additional Power Considerations

As mentioned previously, despite the minute amounts of power that are needed to realize the benefits described, you may want to consider only intermittently stimulating the plants and soil as it will actually increase the performance of your system. Yet, there may be more fundamental reasons to keep the power on intermittently.

In making observations of the formation of root hairs under different conditions, the number and density of root hairs have been known to greatly increase under nutrient stress[214]. This may be a good reason to occasionally turn off the electric field during plant growth to give plants access to the hardships of life, so they can push forward and extend themselves to absorb more nutrients. Even though it may be possible for a plant to electrokinetically come into contact with all of the nutrients it needs to sustain itself, if the plant is not given a reason to reach out and extend its roots into the soil in search of water and nutrients, it will have an adverse effect on the growth and strength of the plant.

The idea of continual versus intermittent stimulation brings up a revelation I had regarding a possible reason for some of the historical failures of electroculture in the late 1930s. If stimulated plants are operating at a much higher efficiency all of the time, day and night, then it seems that the system will eventually break down as the plants' energy stores become depleted without having enough light-energy to sustain the process. Perhaps in the beginning of the systems' operational period, all will be well, but as the stores slowly run out due to energy imbalances, it seems feasible that the plants will eventually lose their vitality. Since it's essential that the plants under stimulation have enough energy to be able to handle the accelerated effects, it's recommended that higher levels of stimulation occur during the daytime, when the

---
[214](Dario et. al, 2008)

plant can compensate for the extra energy expenditure.

To support this hypothesis, consider the historical findings of Spechsnew, who found that the sporadic use of electricity may even be more beneficial compared to continuous use. In contemporary research, one set of experiments performed in Yushu City in Northeast China had very successful results when the electric field was applied once every 10 days (Wang, 2004). When it comes to operation of the system, this may be a good reason to have the system running on a timer for a few hours at a time, once per day, or perhaps once every few days.

Wires

Hook-up Wire

Source: Unicorn Electronics[215]

Wires are used to connect the components together. Since the currents involved are very low, small wires can be used, approximately 20 to 24 AWG[216]. At the same time, depending upon the installation

---
[215] http://www.unicornelex.com/20_Gauge_Black_Red_Zip_Cord_100_Spool_p/22-4516.htm
[216] American Wire Gauge

environment, you don't want to use wires that are too thin, for they tend to be brittle and will not hold up to the wear and tear. For outdoor installations, thicker wires may be better (18 to 20 AWG). Alternatively, you may want to use some low-voltage, waterproof or underground-rated wires that are meant to be used in landscape lighting situations.

For indoor use, you can keep things simple. If you're using a battery charger, you can simply use the wires that it came with.

Electrodes

The electrodes are electrically-conducting materials, which are used to make contact with the soil. While most metals can be used to make a reliable electrical connection to the soil, it turns out that some materials are better than others. Differences in cost, composition and susceptibility to leaching or corrosion are factors that should be considered. In fact, electrodes need not always be metal; they can also be made of conductive, yet inert, materials such as carbon or graphite, or they can be of composite design, consisting of both solid and liquid conductors.

For the sake of this introductory book, you can use just about any commonly available metal as your electrodes, such as a steel bolts or iron nails.

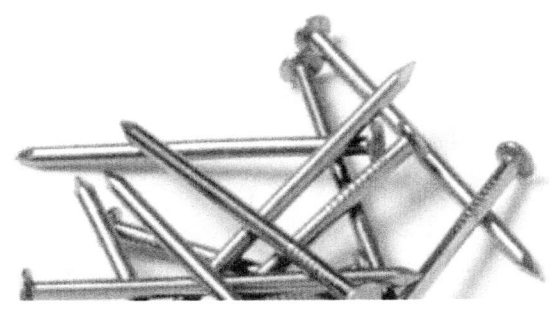

Assorted Nails

Source: IronWireNails.com[217]

> ⚠️ **Warning:**
> Accelerated corrosion will occur upon the application of electric current into the soil. Depending upon the electrode material used, electrolytically-dissociated metal ions can cause soil or plant toxicity problems over time. For this reason, it is best to use electrodes that are non-toxic, e.g. iron-based materials with little or no additives. For some applications, corrosion-resistant steels may also be used. For example, corrosion-resistant stainless steel is a much better material to use compared to copper or aluminum, which can harm the plants and your body, too. Yet, to be fair, even though some materials are resistant, they are not immune to corrosion and when they do corrode, some of their minor elements will be released into the soil. Stainless steel is one example of these types of materials. If it does degrade into the soil, it's helpful to know that the proportion of non-iron impurities (that may be toxic) is generally quite low. Another thing to be aware of is how these metals react to the presence of electricity and the chemicals present within the soil mass. The reason stainless steels may be good in some applications but not others is because some forms of stainless steel produce reaction products, called oxidation compounds, that are toxic. This is a complex topic and further research is needed in this area.

One thing you can do to reduce the amount of electrically-induced corrosion is to use the lowest effective operating voltage that you can. This is because the rate of metal leaching or dissociation is proportional to the voltage used. The greater the voltage, the greater

---

[217] http://www.ironwirenails.com/commonnaillist/nailslist-2.html

the speed of reaction. If the reaction speed is low, it gives time for any potentially harmful reaction products to become diluted within the soil mass.

> It's worth noting that many different soils, especially in urban or developed areas, or in regions where mining may have taken place, already have some of these toxic elements present. The US Environmental Protection Agency has established guidelines as to what levels of heavy metals and other toxic products are considered safe (usually in parts per million). The point of mentioning this here is that while some amounts of toxic release may be okay, it should be avoided. On the other hand, if it cannot be avoided, there are things that you can do to clean up the soil afterwards, e.g. phytoremediation.

Electrode Sizes

If you're planning on using nails or screws, they have a very low cross-sectional area. This means that in small-scale systems, the amount of current or current-density that will be transported through the soil is going to be, for the most part, concentrated along the path directly between both electrodes. In addition to the main flow, there will also be weaker field flows that will come off from the sides of the main conductive path. Depending upon the size of area that needs electrification, it may be better to use larger-sized electrodes to help guarantee that a full-strength electric field is projected through the rhizosphere. This would likely improve the system's efficiency since a larger portion of the root area would be exposed to the electric field.

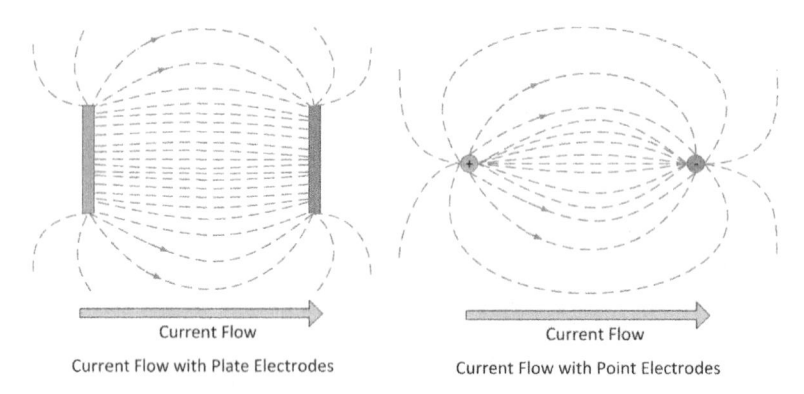

Current Flow with Plate Electrodes   Current Flow with Point Electrodes

Plate vs. Point Electrodes

Because the soil is a non-homogeneous medium, the exact path of the electric field will vary depending upon the best electrical path through the entire soil mass. Furthermore the field will change over time with respect to rock placement, stray metals, moisture levels, soil movement, bacterial influences, root movement, and many other factors.

Assembly

Putting together the system is easy! Just follow the steps below:

Power Supply Preparation

To prepare a standard consumer-electronic power supply for use, there are two simple steps:

1. Remove the power connector at the end of the cord using wire cutters.

Chapter 13: Try It Yourself! 167

Removing the Power Connector

1. Then, remove approximately two inches of plastic insulation from the end of the wire using a wire stripping tool. To do this, use the set-screw to configure the tool to the correct gauge of wire (you can take a guess here), or just do it by 'feel'. It's okay if you make a mistake here since you have lots of wire to play with.

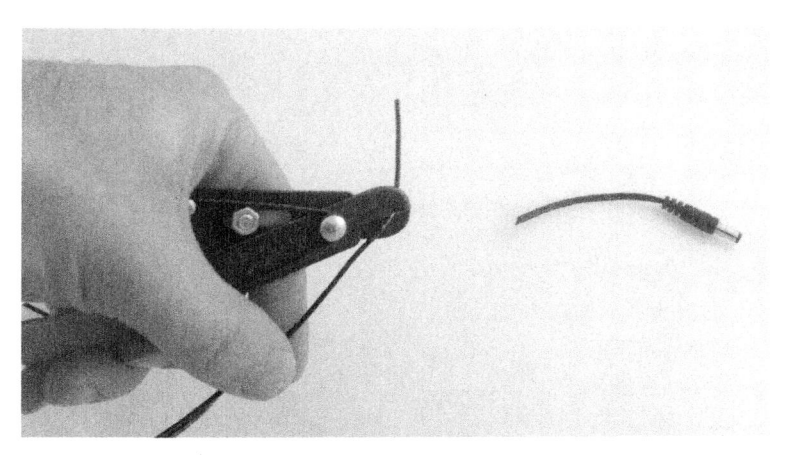

Removing Wire Insulation

The idea is to make an initial cut to get down to the bare wire.

⚠️

Exposing Bare Wire Underneath

Then pull towards the end of the wire to remove everything to the end.

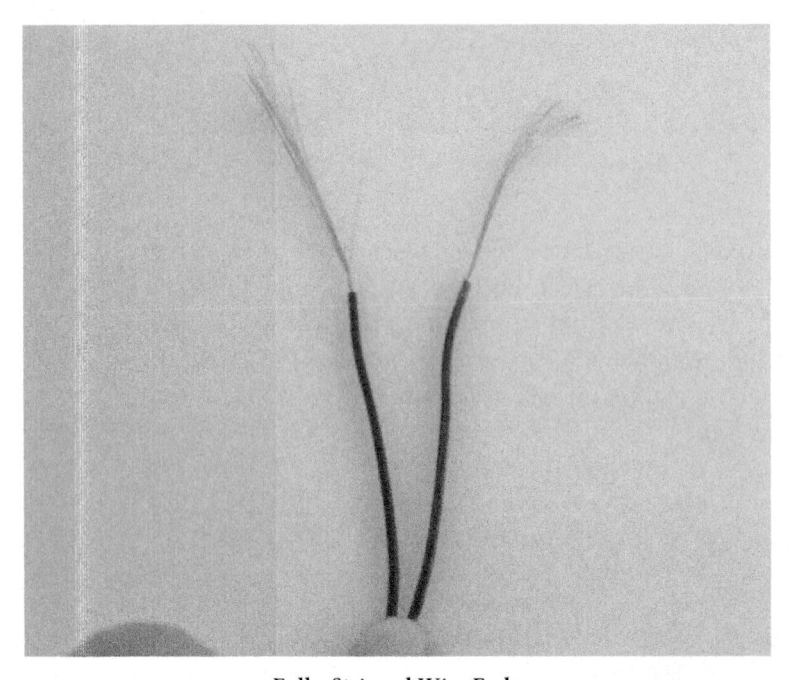

Fully-Stripped Wire Ends

Finally, use your fingers to twist the wires around themselves to create a wire-bundle.

Chapter 13: Try It Yourself!   169

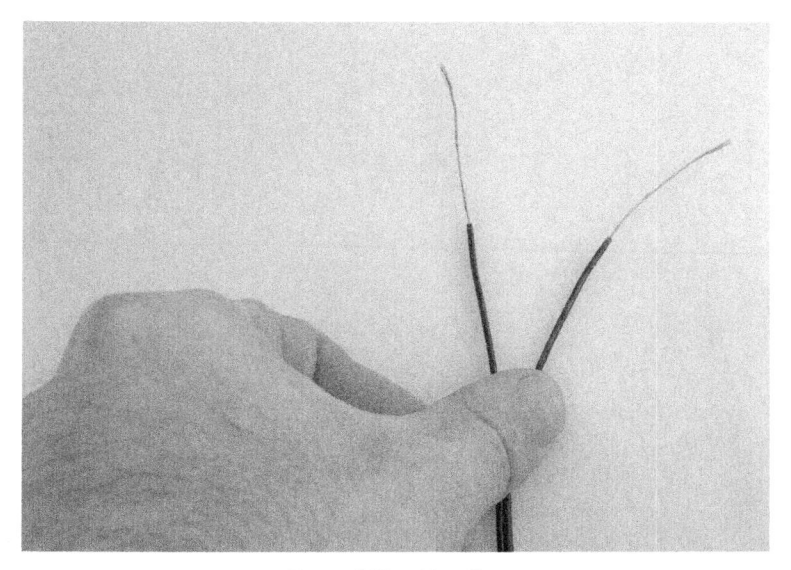

Twisted Wire Bundles

Electrode Preparation and Final Assembly

To attach your power supply to your electrodes, do the following:

If you're using nails or screws, wrap the exposed portions of the wires tightly around the head of each electrode.

1) Begin by wrapping it around the head of the nail 1-2 times, depending upon the length of the exposed wire.

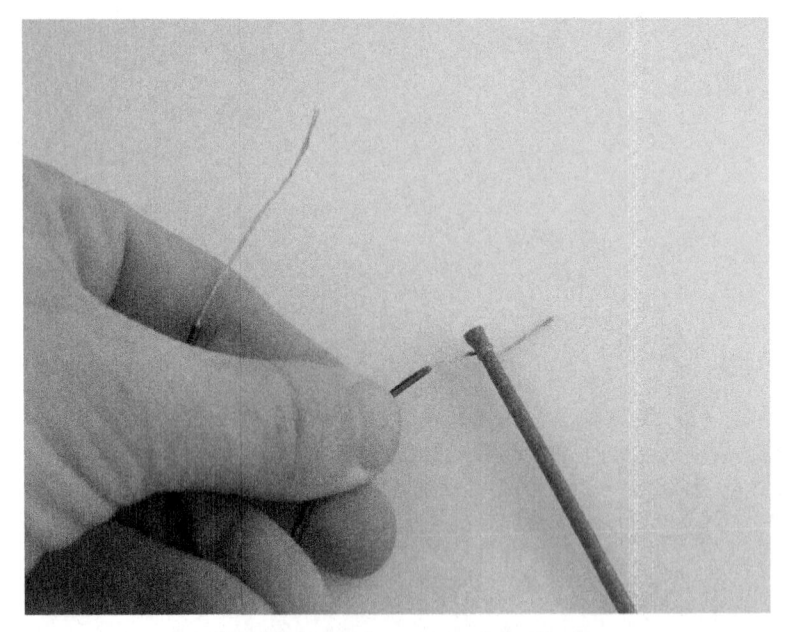

Wire Wrapped Once Around the Head

2) Then, take the excess wire hanging off of the end and wrap it around itself, as shown below. Try to keep things tight to make the connection strong.

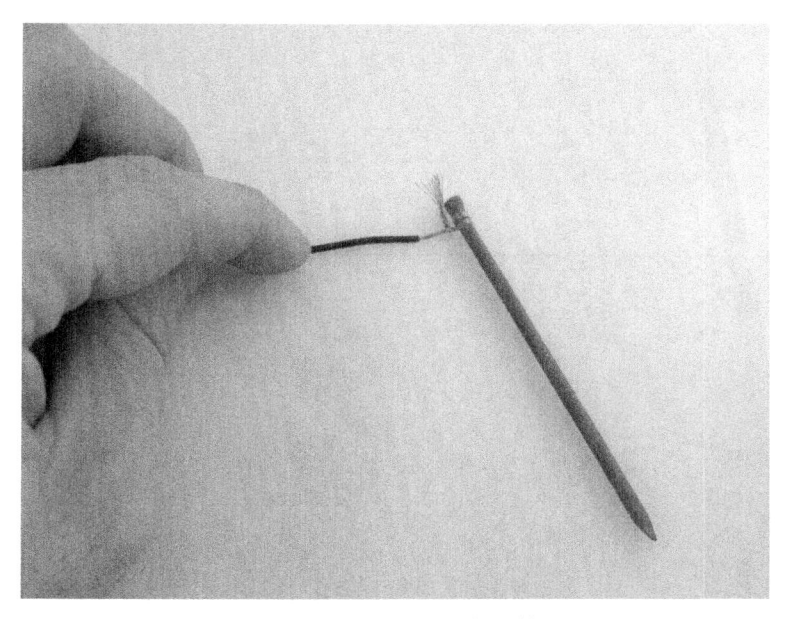

Wire Wrapped Around Itself

When nearing the end of the wire, wrap the wire back around the main wire and twist until tight. If a pair of needle-nose pliers is available, then they can be used to twist the wires more tightly. The finished electrode will look something like this:

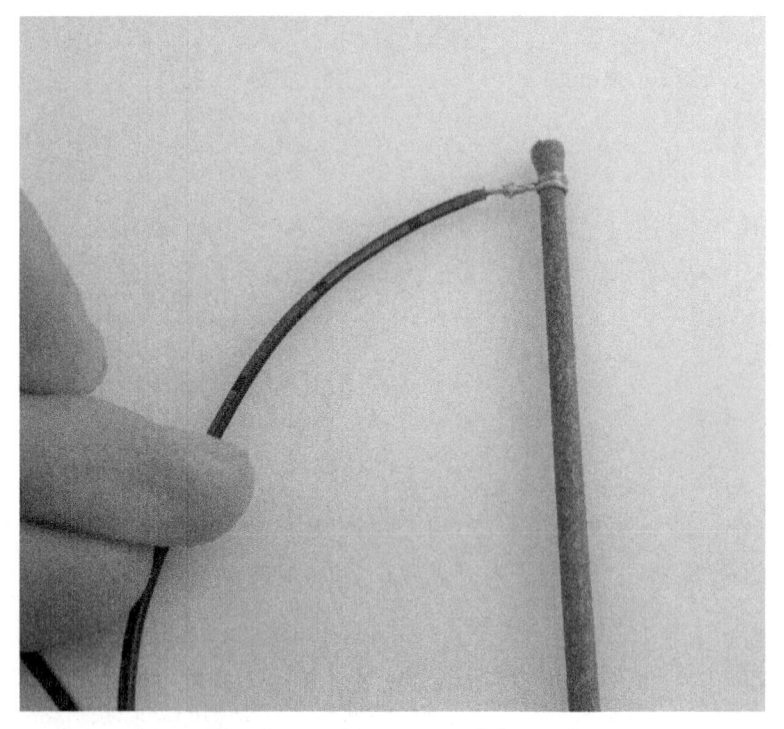

Wire Wrapped Once Around the Head

Do this for both wires.

After you attach each wire to its respective nail, you should have two electrodes wired up. To guarantee the best electrical connection over time, it would be best to solder the wires to the electrode[^FootCordPolarity]. I recommend you check out the following tutorial for more information:

Note: Soldering to a nail or screw, especially a large one, may require lots of heat, in which case using a torch may be better than using a soldering iron.

Chapter 13: Try It Yourself!   173

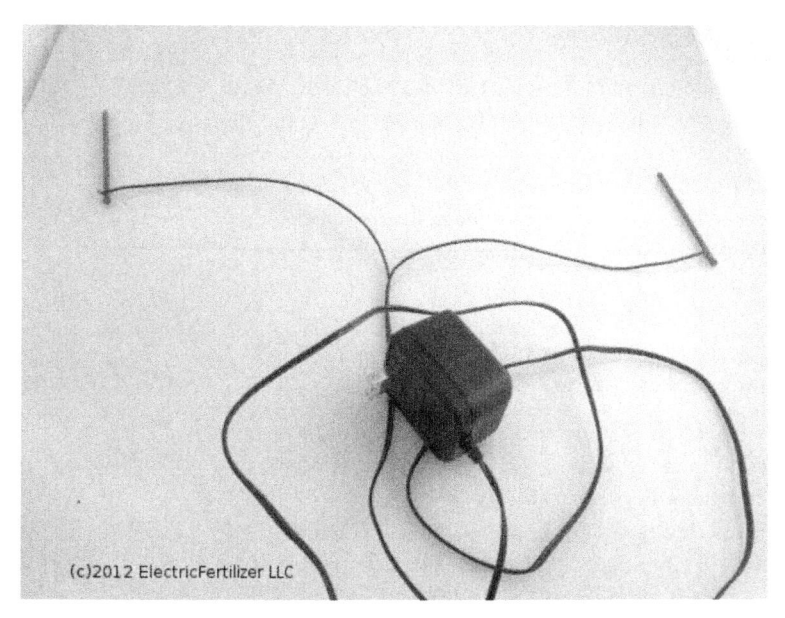

Your Assembled Electroculture System

Troubleshooting Tip

One good reason for having a multimeter is because of a feature called a "conductivity test." In this mode, the device will emit a beep when the probes are touching two points that are electrically connected to each other. This is a great tool to have for troubleshooting problems that may occur when the electrodes look connected, but electrically aren't. This can be due to a number of reasons ranging from mechanical stress (e.g. loose wires from pulling), or corrosion, making for a weak connection.

To give it a try now, while your multimeter is on the continuity test mode, touch one probe to the electrode and the other end to the far end of the wire that's connected to it. If you hear a "beeping" sound, then the electrode and the wire are electrically connected.

If not, then you may need re-solder your wire joint, or possibly re-make the entire electrode assembly.

At this point, your basic electro-horticulture system is complete.

Waterproofing Tip

To extend the life of your electrical connections, you can coat your electrical connections in silicone gel or rubber cement. This will help with keeping moisture out when they get wet from watering or high-humidity.

Installation

Growing in Containers

If you're growing your plants in containers or pots, installation is very easy. Simply place the powered electrodes into the soil on either side of the plant that's being grown. If the container is larger, perhaps up to three feet in length, the electrodes can be placed into the soil on either side of the container, allowing the electric field to penetrate all of the plants in-between.

Growing in the Ground

When it comes to trying out electroculture in the ground, it becomes more complicated. First, the ground is not homogeneous. There will be different amounts and densities of materials present under the ground. Any metals present will distort the electric field, too. Furthermore, from an experimental point of view, the electric field is going to extend beyond your experimental growing area, into the surrounding areas as well.

So if you apply an electric field to the ground, you can not only expect the crops you're growing to be affected, but also the weeds, other plants, and nearby trees to be influenced in one way or another as well. What this means is that it will be very difficult to determine whether your control plants are affected or not because you will not know the extent of the applied electric field.

One way of working around this would be to find two areas that are separated by a large enough distance and perform the experiment in that way. What amount of distance is enough? That's not an easy question to answer since the field will extend in all directions. Factors that need to be considered include the source voltage, electrode arrangement, electrode polarity, soil characteristics and moisture level. This would be an area of experimentation. Once the location of both plots are determined, adjustments should be made to make sure that both plots are as close to being the same as possible. In the outdoor tests I and close associates have performed, we have observed that the field has an effective range of about 10 to 15 feet from the main electrode line (i.e. the line connecting a pair of electrodes).

In-Ground Electrode Configuration

When placing your electrodes into the ground, there are two electrode installation items to consider:

1) Electrode dimensions 2) Distance between electrodes

Electrode Dimensions

When it comes to determining the size of the electrodes you want to use, for simple experiments (e.g. in small containers), the size doesn't really matter that much as long as there is a path for the current to travel through the soil and come into contact with the root system. As mentioned earlier, to get better performance, it would be advisable to use larger surface-area electrodes as they would better guarantee that the electrical current will come into contact with most or possibly the entire root mass of the plants.

It's worth noting that the path that the electricity takes will always be unknown, especially in outdoor soils where soils are generally not consistently mixed, and a variety of objects and ground conditions can cause the electrical current to take varying paths to get to the other side. That's why having a large electrode is beneficial as it helps with offering many more paths to make it to the other side, while also helping to ensure that more biological material is in contact with the electric field.

While the dimensions affect the radiated electric field, they also affect the current density, which by definition is the ratio of current per electrode surface area (i.e. current in Amps / surface area). So generally speaking, a smaller electrode will have a larger current density compared to a larger electrode which can have a much smaller current density. This value may also have an effect on how well plants respond. If a larger voltage is used with a pair of electrodes that have a high current density, it may be harmful to the plant roots. So if adverse results are observed, consider using larger electrodes as well as the operating voltage.

Distance Between Electrodes

When designing your system, if you desire more current (or a larger electric field strength) to be passed through the plant(s), you will need to pay attention to the distance between the electrodes, too. A rule of thumb is that the closer the electrodes are to one another, the stronger the electric field will be. The electric field is the ratio between the applied voltage and the distance between the two electrodes (Voltage / distance). Theoretically, the electric field strength should be constant throughout the region between the electrodes. In reality though, it is going to vary due to the varied electrical conditions that are present.

According to an article by Volkov in Applied Electrical Phenomena[218], the optimal electric field strengths range between 10 mV/m and 10 V/m. In US measurements, the range becomes 3.3 mV/foot to 3.3V/foot. Keep in mind that the electric field strengths that may be the most beneficial will vary depending upon the soil conditions, the type of plant being experimented upon, and the type of electrical stimulation that's involved.

Remember, the early experimenters of electroculture used earth battery technology, which was only capable of producing about 1.3 volts between the plates. Knowing that they had successes with the plates 90 feet apart as well as 200 feet apart, this equates to field strengths of 14mV/ft (48mV/m) and 6mV/ft (21mV/m), respectively.

When electrodes are placed far apart from each other, there is an increase in electrical resistance, dropping the current flow. Since only minute amounts of current flow are needed (on the order

---
[218](Volkov, 1966)

of micro-Amps in some cases), soil resistance is of little concern for the average experimenter. With this in mind, you can try moving the electrodes farther apart to see the extents by which your system will operate. Keep in mind that the greater the distance, the more plants you can grow in between, allowing for greater plant-boosting return on investment.

Additional In Ground Design Considerations

When it comes to designing your in-ground electroculture system, there are a few basic ways to set up your system.

Below are a set of diagrams showing various electrode configurations:

Electrodes on Row Ends

In this configuration, electrodes are placed on opposite ends of a garden row. There are two advantages to this approach: one is that less wiring is involved (though the current will be weaker because the applied field is distributed over a larger area, yet that may be a good thing). The other is that a large number of plants can be grown in between the electrodes. By setting up your garden in this way, you can expect the best returns for minimal effort, compared to setting up electrodes for each plant individually.

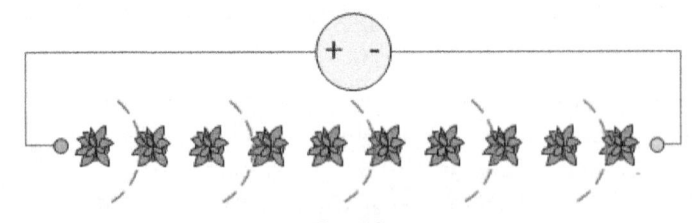

Row Electrification

Electrodes Across Each Plant

When your garden is set up in this approach, electrodes placed on either side of the plant are wired up in parallel producing a stronger electric field upon each individual plant. This comes at greater cost and effort compared to the row end approach. If you want to maintain a higher field strength against each plant, this would be the approach to take.

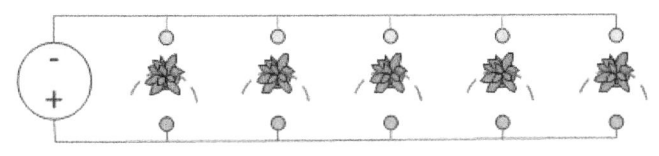

Per Plant Electrification

Electrode Polarity

Direct Plant Stimulation

In cell-culture experiments where only a few cells are grown at a time, cell-growth can be affected by the direction of current flow. One direction of flow can promote growth while the other direction could inhibit it. Keep this in mind when setting up your own direct-stimulation electroculture system. It's important to know what the preferred polarity is for each type of plant, or the effects of the electrical stimulation could be the opposite of those that were intended. The best approach here would be to run preliminary experiments at the same time, at least one for each polarity, to see which one performs better. Depending upon the plant species, the wrong electrical polarity can mean the difference between stunted and improved growth responses.

Soil-based Stimulation

With regards to running experiments in the soil, in the short-term, the polarity doesn't really matter. On the other hand, if you were setting up a system that would be continually powered for an entire season, the long-term effects of one polarity over another may be something to pay attention to. This is important because over time, there is expected to be a lowering of pH near the positive electrode, and this lowered pH region will move towards to negative electrode under the ground, electrokinetically, until equilibrium is reached.

System Operation

All that remains is to turn on the power! If you have other plants to designate as a control group, you should start seeing substantial differences within weeks, assuming the settings are compatible with the plants under test.

One of the first things you'll notice is that your seeds may germinate faster. If you're sowing a number of seeds, you can expect more of them to sprout, as the electric field will increase their chances of germination. After a few weeks, you'll then see longer stems, followed shortly by greener leaves. Remember, the effects that are expressed through electrical stimulation vary by species of plant, their growing environment and possibly by other factors as well. As your plants grow, be sure to make a record of the effects that you observe. More on this in the next chapter.

Soil Moisture Conditions

Keeping the soil moist may seem like the most important task considering that plants need water to survive and, as mentioned earlier, electricity will not flow if the soil is too dry. However, cycles of dry and moist soil can be beneficial. If the soil gets extremely dry, it may limit the flow of electricity, giving the plants a rest from working in an accelerated state. It may also help with giving the roots time to naturally work themselves down to greater depths to search for more water and nutrients.

Remember, this isn't necessarily something to worry about where in the case there is a period of drought, depending upon how the particular plant species reacts, the plants under water-stress may be less susceptible to damage as compared to unelectrified plants.

pH

Most growers know that some plants prefer acidic soils while others prefer more neutral soils. When planting your garden, it's important to know the soil conditions that your plants need for optimal growth.

Due to the electrolytic nature of electroculture, extreme pH conditions may occur at electrode sites. These potential pH hotspots will slowly move from one side of the field to the other. Thus, for people experimenting with large-scale, high-voltage systems where the rates of electrolysis reaction may be significantly faster, it is advised that the active electrodes be placed some distance away from the growing crop, to keep it from being affected by pH extremes. Even under more mild operating conditions, the pH of the soil will likely change over time.

Knowing how sensitive crops can be to pH changes, it would be wise to take some steps ahead of time to prevent acid build-up at the positive electrode by using a buffering agent such as agricultural lime. Another option might be giving the system a rest, allowing time for the soil acids to disperse, especially after a rainfall, which can help push any free hydrogen deeper into the soil mass.

Summary

In this chapter you learned how to assemble your own electro-horticulture system. As you can see, putting a system together is really easy and can be done by anyone with a little time and a few basic materials.

Once your system is together and you start planting seeds, you'll begin to see the effects of electroculture within a couple of weeks, and once you see the benefits with your own eyes, you can start expanding your system by adding additional sets of electrodes, or by varying some of the operating parameters. In the next chapter, we're going to give you some ideas for further experimentation, so you can get really creative with optimizing the growth of your garden.

Chapter 14: Ideas for Further Experimentation

Once you get the hang of the basics of running a system, you may want to start some additional experiments to further your understanding of electroculture. Hands-on experimentation is one of the best ways to learn. With enough experimentation, especially on the variety of plants you that you're already growing, you may be able to move beyond pure experimentation and work towards reliably applying the methods towards your entire garden or farm.

Currently, the state of knowledge on the efficacy of electric fields on different types of food crops is somewhat limited. By joining in our mission to characterize how electric fields work with a variety of plants, you can help growers around the world reap great benefits through the sharing of knowledge and data.

As you can guess, there are innumerable variables that can affect the operation of your experiments. The purpose of this section is to introduce the reader to some of the variables that can be experimented upon.

Questions

It is probably a good idea to start with asking some questions. You may have some questions of your own, but here are some to get you started:

- What method of using electricity results in the fastest growth or the largest yield?

- What is the effect of applying electricity at different times, such as:
- Sowing & germination phase only?
- During main growth?
- Transplants?
- Continuously, day and night?
- Intermittently, such as once an hour, once a day, once a week, and so on?
- Do the types of electrodes used make a difference?
- What materials work best?
- Does it help to use different types or electrode materials at different stages of growth?
- What electrode sizes/dimensions work best along with a particular form of electrical stimuli?
- Which electrode layouts work best?
- At what range?
- At what distance away from the centerline are plants affected by the electric field?
- Does electro-stimulation affect the taste of fruits, vegetables, nuts and grains? What about their size?
- Does electrification affect diseased plants? Which plants? Which diseases?
- Does electrification help protect against insect infestation and damage?

After trying electroculture for a while, can you answer any of these questions yourself? To help you along, below are a number of factors that can be adjusted.

Experimental Variables

Amount of Power

You can experiment with the effect of higher and lower voltages. Does using 9 volts perform better than 5 volts? What about 12 volts?

50 volts? Please be aware that larger amounts of power can be harmful not only to your plants, but also to animals and people, too. Be sure to keep safety in mind. If you have any questions on these matters, it may be worth talking things over with a licensed electrical contractor or engineer.

Time of Electrification

How much time do you need to electrify your plants in order to get beneficial results? What happens if the power is on for long periods of time? Are there any differences? Do all plants respond well to 24/7 stimulation?

For those who want to keep things as natural as possible, it may be worth it to think of the Minimal Effective Dose[219] to get the benefits of stimulation without any of the risks that come from soil or plant over-electrification.

Type of Electrodes

Try out different electrode materials. Despite being somewhat toxic in large quantities, the original experimenters created earth batteries using plates of zinc and copper. Is there a difference from the use of iron versus stainless steel? What about heat-tempered metals? What about other metals such as gold or silver? How does the use of earth batteries compare to using modern power supplies?

How do the electrodes you use fare over time? Do they remain mechanically strong, or do they start looking different? Note that electrodes over time may either develop a thin film-like covering due to electrokinetic adhesion (i.e. electroplating), or they may corrode away, depending upon the polarity, electrode thickness and composition.

Distance Between Electrodes

Since the strength of the electric field is proportional to the distance between the electrodes, consider how close you place your electrodes to each other. With larger voltages, say 12 volts, the system

---

[219] A term coined by Tim Ferriss in his book, *The Four Hour Body*.

should work over larger distances compared to a lower-voltage system over the same distance. Yet remember that the original experimenters of the 18th, 19th and 20th centuries were able to have great success using only 1.3 Volts over distances up to 200 feet. Can 12 volts be used to scale the effective electrode distance up by a factor of 12, to 2400 feet or more?

See what works best. If you use a 12V power supply and the distance is large, do the plants perform better compared to using a lower voltage with electrodes being a shorter distance apart?

Electrode Tips When observing the effects upon the electrodes and the region around them as well, use a voltmeter and ammeter to determine the direction of current flow. Once you know the polarity, for future reference you may want to color one of the wires or electrodes red which usually denotes the positive terminal. Once you know the polarity, you can use a pH meter to monitor the different pH readings that occur at each electrode. For additional help with testing, recommended tools, crop result guidelines and measurement checklists, head over to the ElectricFertilizer Resources page[220] page.

Remember, one electrode gives away ions or electrons and the other receives them. This has multiple effects, not only upon the electrodes themselves, but also on the soil. The changes to the soil include pH changes and electrolysis reactions, especially at the electrodes.

Keep in mind that some materials may not be healthy to use due to electrolytic corrosion, e.g. aluminum, which will put aluminum ions into your soil and the plants that you're growing. It is advised to not use materials that are considered to be toxic to the human body.

---

[220] http://ElectricFertilizer/#resources

Electrical Polarity

Since we now know that plants under direct stimulation (e.g. trees) are affected by the polarity of the electrodes, this can also be a topic of experimentation. Try making the polarity such that the roots are attached to the negative power source terminal and a location someplace higher up in the tree gets connected to the positive terminal. The reverse can also be tested. You can also get creative with using leaves as electrodes, as was done via the "Plantricity" system (deprecated website) that used metal planting pots to apply electricity between different parts of plants to cause large improvements in growth.

Plant Species

The forefathers of this technology experimented with a variety of fruits, vegetables and grains, and they found that some species are likely to be more responsive than others. If you don't have success using the system with one variety of tomato, consider trying other varieties. How do they compare?

By Soil Type

While it is true that electroculture works best in soils with some clay content due to the smaller pore spaces, it has been found to work in a variety of other soils. Try it on whatever is most convenient for you.

Summary

By testing out the many aspects of electrical application on plant systems and sharing the results with each other, we can collectively come to a better understanding of how to best use electroculture for everyone's benefit.

In this chapter we covered many ways that systems can be adjusted or modified to try to produce optimized results. Remember, plant varieties respond differently to different forms of stimulation, so it pays to experiment and try out new things.

If you decide to give electro-horticulture a try, be sure to join our email newsletter[221] and reply with a note and telling us all about it! We may want to talk with you to learn more, or possibly share your experiment or pictures on the our website!

---

[221] http://ElectricFertilizer/#contact

Chapter 15: Conclusion

> "Electrocultural techniques are fully compatible with organic, ecological, and biodynamic methods of growing." - Jeffery Goss Jr., Missouri, USA

Technological innovations like electro-horticulture are capable of greatly improving our ability to not only assist with healing the lands that we've polluted over the years, but to also feed and heal mankind. Before we wrap things up, I'd like to share my vision for electroculture, based on everything I've learned so far.

Natural Organic Growth Stimulation

I'd like to begin by mentioning why it is important to consider the use of electricity-based or even electromagnetic forms of crop stimulation. For starters, it's as natural as you can get - electricity is everywhere! It's in the air, it's in the ground, and through the way atomic physics, chemistry and biology work, nature makes use of built-in and "stray" geo-electrical sources stimulate life into sustaining or accelerating growth. As far as electroculture is concerned at its fundamental level, it's as "organic" as you can get because there's nothing artificial about it; it's just pure energy, like that of a lightning storm.

Using electricity as a stimulation agent puts the burden of "activation" upon the plant itself, rather than through the use of externally-applied amendments, natural or otherwise. Assuming that the form of stimulation correctly matches a plant or crop's needs, it's up to the plant to respond in such a way to create the chemical/hormone/protein synthesis reactions needed to develop these new growth patterns. So what this means is that by just applying a little extra electromagnetic energy to plants or their surrounding environment, we can encourage plants to put their best foot (er, root) forward.

A Vision for the Future of Electroculture

In my vision, I see electroculture as being capable of improving many facets of agriculture. I'd like to begin by revisiting the application ideas listed in the latter portion of the book, as I think it's in the way that we use technology that best defines how we can bring about benevolent change in more sustainable way than has been previously done.

Fertilizer Conservation

A large problem for many farms is the lack of high-quality topsoil that's porous, rich and full of nutrients, humus, soil fungi, and microbes. Fields that have been over-worked for generations and depleted of most of their nutrient bases are now being replaced with commercial fertilizer mixes ranging from general purpose mixes, to specialized applications of anhydrous ammonia, to even, prescribed perfect-fit doses of most everything that's needed, with the advent of precision agriculture technology.

Except for the permaculturalists, most growers are not likely going to move away from the use of fertilizers or other soil amendments. While it's well known that plants only use a portion of what's made available to them, the remaining portions of which are typically left on the land to be used in subsequent planting cycles or more predominantly, are washed away into ground-water supplies or top-soil runoff into nearby lakes and streams. The over-fertilization of farmland is a cause of many environmental problems ranging from algae blooms to phosphorous poisoning.

Using electroculture as an engineered approach could improve this situation. It would do so by providing a way to either reduce or even eliminate the need for external fertilization inputs. In the case that a full dose of inputs are still used, it can help with greatly improving its utilization efficiency, making the best use of everything that's been added. Furthermore, since soils may also contain natural bio-remediation or toxic-waste-consuming bacteria, electrified soils can help with converting toxic excess into benign byproducts that may no longer cause long-term harm to plants or other organisms in the food chain.

Remote Farming

In places where farming is performed not only as a means for making a living, but also for basic survival, improving the fertility of soils without using any physical inputs can be a great advantage over the logistic hardships present in remote locations.

For example, a grower from high in the Andes Mountains or in the middle of nowhere may want to find a way to improve their crop, perhaps in terms of yield improvements or to help bring forth needed traits like drought resistance. A great way to do this would be through electroculture. Not only will these systems be relatively inexpensive to implement, but more importantly, they will drastically reduce or even negate the need for shipped-in fertilizer inputs. Work can also be reduced over the long term by electrokinetically moving nutrients around through the soil itself.

Elimination of Artificial Growth Hormones

Some growers have been using artificial hormones to achieve many of the beneficial effects noted here. These hormones can be synthesized externally, or can be bred into plants via genetic manipulation (i.e. GMOs). While the effects of synthetic hormones and enzymes are scientifically proven as being very effective, there is a growing movement worldwide questioning the long-term health effects from the use of these technologies.

If instead these were naturally stimulated into existence from the plant's own biological chemical-producing processes, their synthesis and use may be better regulated, reducing or preventing possible health side-effects from the alternative. Natural is usually better.

Handling Climate Change

As covered earlier, the potential exists for using electroculture to help protect crops against climate problems ranging from unforeseen early frost damage to increased occurrences of drought. By offering a solution that can help growers who can't afford complex irrigation systems, or those who struggle even to find water sources, electroculture can offer some help in this area. For instance, one grower of tomatoes reported that during multiple trials, the electrified group of plants consumed significantly less water than the un-electrified group.

Having additional buffer time available may mean the difference between life and death, feast or famine.

Accelerated Cleansing of the Earth

Humanity has done a lot of damage to planet Earth, the environment, many wildlife habitats, and many of our food and medicine sources as well.

While environmental cleaning technology, also known as remediation technology, has become an entire engineering field of its own, cleanup often requires big money contracts or large organizations capable of driving these technology efforts.

In contrast to using heavy machinery to remove large amounts of soil, cleaning it up through various means, and then returning it to the excavation site, the use of natural processes like bioremediation and phytoremediation can be used to clean up these problems for little or no cost. Using electroculture, these methods can even be accelerated, cleaning up more, faster.

I envision that a new movement can be created (assuming it doesn't already exist), where individuals are empowered to take on environmental cleanup tasks without needing to rely on big-money projects. This is especially necessary for those who are unable to afford the cleanup or for wildlife areas outside of the reach of heavy-equipment-based cleaning crews.

Some areas, such as India's extremely populated sea freighter dismantling and electronics recycling areas, are rich in extremely toxic heavy metals and chemical carcinogens. Teaching people in these regions about the benefits of planting fields of hyperaccumulating plants could help immensely in decontaminating the land they reside on. Accelerating the process using low-cost, locally-sourced electroculture systems could then, over a much shorter period of time than usual, create a safer place to for people to live and raise families.

With electro-horticulture, all of this is possible and more!

Thank You

Thank you for taking the time to read this book. I hope you find inspiration from it and start experimenting yourself! If you have any questions at all, feel free to contact me at ElectricFertilizer.com[222]!

Furthermore, to learn more, Join our email newsletter[223] where you'll receive tips and tricks, case studies, and the occasional

---
[222] http://ElectricFertilizer.com/#contact
[223] http://ElectricFertilizer.com/#contact

product offering that will make trying out electroculture much easier than cobbling a system together.

Reviews Welcome!

As a final request, if you enjoyed reading this book, consider leaving us a 5-star review and a comment on the platform that you purchased us with.

Thanks again & Happy Experimenting!

Appendix: Get Involved

Make Some Discoveries

In this way you can help progress the cutting edge of electric agriculture.

> ### Get More!
>
> Sign up for the ElectricFertilizer.com[a] newsletter today for the latest news and discoveries, success stories, operating tips, helpful products, and more.
>
> Check out the website for upcoming products that will make this new form of gardening even easier to try out. Look out for kits, books, and other resources to push your garden to the max!
>
> ---
> [a] https://electricfertilizer.com/#contact

Glossary

A

Action potential
An action potential is a short-lasting electrophysical event in which the electrical membrane potential (i.e. voltage) of a cell rapidly rises and then falls.

Active transport
Active transport methods (e.g. using carrier proteins) that are used for pumping molecules or ions against a concentration gradient, i.e. from low concentration to a high concentration.

Adsorbed
Is the adhesion of atoms, ions, or molecules from a gas, liquid, or dissolved solid to a surface, creating a film. As a result from electrolysis reactions within the soil, it is expected that some charged compounds naturally found within the soil will be adsorbed onto the electrode of the opposite electrical charge, e.g. Positive sodium ions from the breakup of salt may attach themselves to the negative electrode.

Aeroculture
A method of growing plants without soil by suspending them above sprays that constantly moisten the roots with water and nutrients. The advantage of this method is that roots are exposed to high amounts of atmospheric oxygen.

Ammeter
An ammeter is an electronic measurement device used to measure electrical current in units of Amperes or Amps.

Glossary

Anode
    The positive electrode terminal.

Apiarist
    A person who keeps an apiary, aka a beekeeper.

ATP In biochemistry, is short for Adenosine Triphosphate, and serves as a source of energy for various physiological reactions, as in active-transport.

B

Bioremediation
    The use of plants to extract heavy metals from contaminated soils and water. Also called phytoremediation.

Brownfield
    An industrial or commercial site that is idle or underused due to environmental pollution

C

Callus
    No, we're not talking about mean people here... In botany, a callus refers to a mass of unorganized cells. These cells grow in response to different forms of stimuli, e.g. wounding-response. Some good information can be found in this paper[224].

Cathode
    The negative electrode terminal.

Cellular depolarization
    Under normal circumstances, the internal charge of a biological cell is negatively charged with respect to its surrounding environment. In the process of depolarization, the cell's charge becomes positive for a very brief period of time.

---
[224] http://www.ncbi.nlm.nih.gov/pmc/articles/PMC3809525/

Channel proteins

These are structures found within the cell membrane that allow for the transport (controlled or uncontrolled) of ions or other substances into or out of a cell. An example is the Ion Channel. More information can be found via Wikipedia[225].

Chemical diffusion

Is the net movement of a substance (e.g. an atom, ion, or molecule) from a region of high concentration to a region of low concentration.

Chloroplasts

Are organelles (akin to thinking of organs within a body) - membrane-bound structures found within a cell whose main role is to conduct photosynthesis. In photosynthesis, the pigment chlorophyll captures energy from sunlight and stores it in energy storage molecules while freeing oxygen from water. See Wikipedia[226] for more information.

Colloids

Are substances in which microscropically dispersed insoluble particles are suspended throughout another substance. Sub-types include aerosols (smoke), gels (aerogel), emulsions (mayonannaise) and foams (shaving cream).

Concentration gradient

The gradual difference in concentration of a dissolved substance in a solution between a region of high density and one of lower density. (via reference.com)

Control group

Is separated from the rest of the experiment, whereas it is not part of the main test. A typical control group does not receive any treatment compared to that of the experimental group(s).

---

[225] http://en.wikipedia.org/wiki/Ion_channel
[226] http://en.wikipedia.org/wiki/Chloroplast

D

Desorption
Is a phenomenon where by a substance is released from or through a surface. (Via Wikipedia)[227]

Differentiation
Is a process by which a less specialized cell becomes a more specialized cell type. (via Wikipedia)[228]

DNA
Short for the molecule deoxyribonucleic acid, it encodes genetic instructions used in the development and functioning of all known living organisms. (via Wikipedia)[229]

E

Electrical current
Is a flow of electric charge, often carried by electrons moving within a wire, or ions moving within an electrolyte. (via Wikipedia)[230]

Electric field
Is generated by electric charge and time-varying magnetic fields. It describes an electric force experienced by motionless test particle at a point in space. They contain electrical energy. Learn more at Wikipedia[231].

Electrochemical gradient
Is composed of two parts, an electric potential (voltage) and a

---

[227] http://en.wikipedia.org/wiki/Desorption
[228] http://en.wikipedia.org/wiki/Cellular_differentiation
[229] http://en.wikipedia.org/wiki/DNA
[230] http://en.wikipedia.org/wiki/Electric_current
[231] http://en.wikipedia.org/wiki/Electric_field

difference in chemical concentration across a membrane. (via Wikipedia)[232]

Electromigration
Is the transport of material caused by the gradual movement of ions in a conductor (or conducting medium, like moist soil), due to the momentum transfer between conducting electrons and diffusing atoms. (via Wikipedia)[233]

Electroosmosis
A bulk transport of water, which flows through the soil as a result of the applied electrical field. The flow of liquid is induced by an applied voltage across a porous material. (via Wikipedia)[234]

Electrophoresis
The movement of charged particles and colloids under the influence of an electrical field. As an example, in electroculture or electrokinetic remediation activities, negatively-charged clay particles or cellular organisms are transported towards a positive electrode located within the soil mass.

Electrotonic potential
A fast-moving signaling effect that occurs within cells in reaction to cellular depolarization where charge collections start moving to different portions of the cell wall. See: (Kahn Academy](http://www.khanacademy.org/science/biology/human-biology/v/electrotonic-and-action-potentials] for a great explanation.

F

Facilitated diffusion
Is the transport of ions or molecules across a biological

---

[232] http://en.wikipedia.org/wiki/Electrochemical_gradient
[233] http://en.wikipedia.org/wiki/Electromigration
[234] http://en.wikipedia.org/wiki/Electro-osmosis

Glossary 201

membrane via specific membrane proteins located within the cell wall. (via Wikipedia)[235]

Fungal hyphae
Refers to a long, branching filamentous structure of a fungus. They are the main mode of vegetative growth and are collectively called a mycelium. (via Wikipedia)[236]

H

Homogeneous
Refers to substances, like soil, being of uniform structure or composition.

Hydrolysis
Refers to the cleavage of chemical bonds by the addition of water.

Hydroxyl ion
Is a chemical functional group containing an oxygen atom connected to a hydrogen atom by a covalent bond. (via Wikipedia)[237]

Hydrogen ion
Is strictly speaking, the nucleus of a hydrogen atom separated from its accompanying electron. It's also known as a proton. (via Britannica)[238]

I

---
[235] http://en.wikipedia.org/wiki/Facilitated_diffusion
[236] http://en.wikipedia.org/wiki/Hypha
[237] http://en.wikipedia.org/wiki/Hydroxyl
[238] http://www.britannica.com/EBchecked/topic/278733/hydrogen-ion

In-situ
Is a Latin phrase that means in-place or on-site. (via Wikipedia)[239]

Ion pumps
Is a transmembrane protein that moves ions across a plasma membrane against their concentration gradient. (via Wikipedia)[240]

K

Kaolinite
Is a clay mineral that naturally occurs in soils that have formed from the chemical weathering of rocks in hot, moist climates, e.g. tropical rainforests. (via Wikipedia)[241]

L

Lipid bilayer
Is a thin polar membrane made of two layers of lipid molecules. They form a continuous barrier around all cells or almost all living organisms. (via Wikipedia)[242]

M

Membrane potential
Is the difference in electric potential (voltage) between the interior and the exterior of a biological cell. (via Wikipedia)[243]

Metabolite
Are the intermediates and products of metabolism. They have various functions including fuel, structure, signaling, stimulatory, etc. (via Wikipedia)[244]

---

[239] http://en.wikipedia.org/wiki/In_situ
[240] http://en.wikipedia.org/wiki/Ion_transporter
[241] http://en.wikipedia.org/wiki/Kaolinite
[242] http://en.wikipedia.org/wiki/Lipid_bilayer
[243] http://en.wikipedia.org/wiki/Membrane_potential
[244] http://en.wikipedia.org/wiki/Metabolite

Glossary

N

Negative membrane resting potential
　　Is the state that an electrically-sensitive cell resides in before the build-up of electrical charge occurs on the way towards causing an action-potential event.

O

Oxidation
　　Describes the loss of electrons by a molecule, atom or ion. (via Wikipedia)[245]

P

Passive-transport
　　Is the movement of biochemicals and other atomic or molecular substances across cell membranes, without the use of chemical energy. (via Wikipedia)[246]

R

Root exudates
　　Refers to fluids emitted by an organism through pores. It is known that plant roots emit various chemicals that may be beneficial or harmful to surrounding plants, as used in the case of companion planting. (via Wikipedia)[247]

Redox reactions
　　Includes all chemical reactions in which atoms have their oxidation state changed. Examples include the oxidation of carbon to yield carbon dioxide, or the reduction of carbon by hydrogen to yield methane. (via Wikipedia)[248]

---
[245] http://en.wikipedia.org/wiki/Redox
[246] http://en.wikipedia.org/wiki/Passive_transport
[247] http://en.wikipedia.org/wiki/Exudate
[248] http://en.wikipedia.org/wiki/Redox

Reduction
Describes the gain of electrons by a molecule, atom or ion. (via Wikipedia)[249]

Remediation
Deals with the removal of pollution or contaminants from environmental media such as soil or groundwater. See more at Wikipedia[250]

RNA
Refers to a family of large biological molecules that perform multiple vital roles in the coding, decoding, regulation, and expression of genes. (via Wikipedia)[251]

S

Sediment
Is a naturally occurring material that is broken down by processes of weathering and erosion, and subsequently transported by environmental forces. (via Wikipedia)[252]

Succession plants
Refers to an phenomenon or process by which an ecological community undergoes more or less orderly and predictable changes following a disturbance or initial colonization of a new habitat. Disturbances can be fire or excessive logging, etc. First-succession plants refers to pioneer plants like mosses, grasses, small shrubs and trees. (via Wikipedia)[253]

T

---

[249] http://en.wikipedia.org/wiki/Redox
[250] http://en.wikipedia.org/wiki/Environmental_remediation
[251] http://en.wikipedia.org/wiki/RNA
[252] http://en.wikipedia.org/wiki/Sediment
[253] http://en.wikipedia.org/wiki/Ecological_succession

Transpiration
Is the process of water movement through a plant and its evaporation from leaves, stems and flowers. (via Wikipedia)[254]

V

VOCs
Short for Volatile Organic Compounds, these are essentially gaseous organic compounds (e.g. odors) that are emitted from a various solids or liquids. Examples range from green leaf volatiles (e.g. plant phermones, or signaling compounds that are released after a plant wounding event) to hazardous chemicals that off-gas from paints and other coatings. (via Wikipedia)[255]

Voltage gated channels
Are a class of transmembrane ion channels that are activated by changes in electrical membrane voltage near the channel. These types of ion channels are especially critical in neurons, but are common in many types of cells. (via Wikipedia)[256]

---
[254] http://en.wikipedia.org/wiki/Transpiration
[255] http://en.wikipedia.org/wiki/Volatile_organic_compound
[256] http://en.wikipedia.org/wiki/Voltage-gated_ion_channel

Bibliography

A

Acar, Yalcin B., Akram N. Alshawabkeh, and Randy A. Parker. 1997. Theoretical and Experimental Modeling of Multi-species Transport in Soils Under Electric Fields Project Summary /. Cincinnati, OH: U.S. Environmental Protection Agency, National Risk Management Research Laboratory.

Acuna, Adrian J., Oscar H. Pucci, and Graciela N. Pucci. 2012. "Electrobioremediation of Hydrocarbon Contaminated Soil from Patagonia Argentina." In New Technologies in the Oil and Gas Industry, edited by Jorge Salgado Gomes. InTech. link[257]

Agulova, L.P. and A.M, Opalinskaya, "Analysis of Weak Magnetic Field Effects on the Piccardi Test and the Belousov-Zhabotinsky Reaction" link[258]

Alshawabkeh, Akram N. 2001. "Short CourseBasics and Applications of Electrokinetic Remediation". Course Notes November 19, Federal University of Rio de Janeiro. link[259]

Arcinue, A. E.;Rillon. 1982. "Growth and yield performance of bush sitao using the electrogenic crop stimulation system [Philippines]." CLSU Scientific Journal 3 (1) (October): p. 69–74.

Artemis, Barinov, THE EFFECT OF ELECTRICITY ON PLANT GROWTH, Moscow College, Moscow, 2012, link[260]

Artemis, Barinov, THE EFFECT OF ELECTRICITY ON PLANT

---

[257] http://www.intechopen.com/books/new-technologies-in-the-oil-and-gas-industry/electrobioremediation-of-hydrocarbon-contaminated-soil-from-patagonia-argentina
[258] http://www.amazon.com/Geo-Cosmic-Relations-Macro-Environment-Proceedings-International/dp/9022010066
[259] http://www.scribd.com/doc/70772833/alshawabkeh-shortcourse
[260] http://sch35-2007.narod.ru/itogi_conf_2012/1_Barinov_1535.pdf

GROWTH, Moscow College, Moscow, 2012, link[261]

B

Stone, G.E., Cyclopedia of American Agriculture, Vol 2: Crops. 1911, Macmillan. link[262]

Berg, H., Zhang, L., Electrostimulation in Cell Biology by Low-Frequency Electromagnetic Fields, Electromagnetic Biology and Medicine 1993 12:2, 147-163 link[263]

Black, J. D., F. R. Forsyth, D. S. Fensom, and R. B. Ross. 1971. "Electrical Stimulation and Its Effects on Growth and Ion Accumulation in Tomato Plants." Canadian Journal of Botany 49 (10) (October): 1809–1815. doi:10.1139/b71-255.

Bollen, Walter Beno. 1959. Microorganisms and Soil Fertility. Oregon State Monographs. Studies in Bacteriology,no. 1. Corvallis: Oregon State College. link[264]

Bowker, George E., and Hugh C. Crenshaw. 2007. "Electrostatic Forces in wind-pollination—Part 2: Simulations of Pollen Capture." Atmospheric Environment 41 (8) (March): 1596–1603. doi:10.1016/j.atmosenv.2006.10.048. link[265]

Brady, Steve, Master Gardener Hour, 5/19/12.

Briggs, Campbell, Heald and Flint, Department Bulletin No. 1379, United States Department of Agriculture, Washington DC, January 1926, p.18-19

Burns, John T., Cosmic Influences on Humans, Animals, and Plants: An Annotated Bibliography link[266]

Byers, T.J. 1984. "How a Solar Root Stimulator Can Help Grow

---

[261] http://sch35-2007.narod.ru/itogi_conf_2012/1_Barinov_1535.pdf
[262] http://books.google.com/books?id=IjiucRg4skwC
[263] http://informahealthcare.com/action/showCitFormats?doi=10.3109%2F15368379309012869
[264] http://catalog.hathitrust.org/Record/009111200
[265] http://www.sciencedirect.com/science/article/pii/S1352231006010752
[266] http://books.google.com/books?id=AUoYWVdTUhEC&lpg=PA161&ots=x14gk1X40c&dq=faraday's%20cage%20plants&pg=PA113#v=onepage&q=plants&f=false

Healthy Plants - Organic Gardening - MOTHER EARTH NEWS." Mother Earth News. link[267]

C

Carlson, Neil. A. (1992), *Foundations of Physiological Psychology*, Needham Heights, Massachusetts: Simon & Schuster, pp. 55.

Chen Hua, and Wu JunLin. 2009. "Different electric field strength treatment of buckwheat seeds and biological effect of buckwheat seedling under drought stress." Research of Agricultural Modernization 30 (3): 381–384. CABDirect2.

Chopra, Surinder, and Max Fomitchev-Zamilov. "Investigation of the Effects of Electrostatic and Magnetostatic Treatment on Plants Growths and Their Genetic Composition". Quantum Potential Corporation, State College, PA 16803.

Chrispeels, Maarten J., Nigel M. Crawford, and Julian I. Schroeder. 1999. "Proteins for Transport of Water and Mineral Nutrients Across the Membranes of Plant Cells." The Plant Cell Online 11 (4) (4–1): 661–675. doi:10.1105/tpc.11.4.661. link[268]

Christofleau, Justin. 1927. Electroculture. Perth, Western Australia: Alex. Trouchet & Son.

D

Dario, Paolo, Cecilia Laschi, Barbara Mazzolai, Paolo Corradi, Virgilio Mattoli, Alessio Mondini, Stefano Mancuso, et al. 2008. "Bio-inspiration from Plants' Roots Final Report Plant-inspired robots for planetary exploration (SeedBot)". European Space Agency. link[269]

Desrosiers, M F, and R S Bandurski. 1988. "Effect of a Longitudinally Applied Voltage Upon the Growth of Zea Mays Seedlings." Plant Physiology 87: 874–877.

Dhital, Shambhu P., Hak Tae Lim, and Buddhi P. Sharma. 2008.

---
[267] http://www.motherearthnews.com/organic-gardening/root-stimulator.aspx?page=2
[268] http://www.plantcell.org/content/11/4/661
[269] http://www.esa.int/gsp/ACT/doc/ARI/ARI%20Study%20Report/ACT-RPT-BIO-ARI-066301-SeedBot-PisaFirenze.pdf

"Electrotherapy and Chemotherapy for Eliminating Double-Infected Potato Virus (PLRV and PVY) from In Vitro Plantlets of Potato (Solanum Tuberosum L.)." HORTICULTURE ENVIRONMENT and BIOTECHNOLOGY 49 (1) (February): 52–57. link[270]

Dorchester, Charles S. 1889-1937. The Effect of Electric Current on Certain Crop Plants /. Research Bulletin; Agricultural Experiment Station, Iowa State College of Agriculture and Mechanic Arts, p9.

DuBois, Marc L. 2010. Action Potential: Biophysical and Cellular Context, Initiation, Phases, and Propagation. 1st ed. Nova Science Publishers.

Dudareva, Natalia, and Eran Pichersky. 2008. "Metabolic Engineering of Plant Volatiles." Current Opinion in Biotechnology 19 (2) (April): 181–189. doi:10.1016/j.copbio.2008.02.011. p2-3 link[271]

E

Ennis, Matthew. 2012. Personal Gmail account. "You Had Some Questions for Me."

F

E. Ferrarese, Electrochemical Oxidation of Soils Contaminated with Organic Pollutants, Trento: Dipartimento di Ingegneria Civile e Ambientale, 2008, 282 p. - (Monographs of the Doctoral School in Environmental Engineering; 11). - ISBN: 978-88-8443-245-2. - Tesi di dottorato in formato elettronico

G

Gish, O. H. (1936a). Electrical messages from the Earth, their reception and interpretation,]. Wash. Acad. Sci. 26, 267-289. Gish, O. H. (1936b). Electrical messages from the Earth, their reception and interpretation, Sci. Mon. N. Y. 43, 47-57.

Goldsworthy, Andrew. 1986. "The Electric Compass of Plants." New

---

[270] http://www.dbpia.co.kr/Article/794863
[271] http://www.mcdb.lsa.umich.edu/labs/pichersky/references/Metabolicengineeringofplantvolatiles.pdf

Scientist, January 2.

Goldsworthy, Andrew. 2006. "Effects of Electrical and Electromagnetic Fields on Plants and Related Topics." In Plant Electrophysiology, edited by Alexander G. Volkov, 247–267. Berlin, Heidelberg: Springer Berlin Heidelberg. link[272]

Goldsworthy, Andrew. "Home Page of Dr. A. Goldsworthy". University Professor Home Page. Dr A Goldsworthy, Plant Biotechnology. link[273]

Goodsell, D.S. 2004. "The Calcium Pump." RCSB Protein Data Bank (March 1). doi:10.2210/rcsb_pdb/mom_2004_3. link[274]

Goss Jr., Jeffrey. "Grow Healthier Crops: The Art & Science of Electroculture." link[275]

Guardiola, Jose L., INCREASING CITRUS FRUIT SIZE WITH SYNTHETIC AUXINS, Departamento de Biologia Vegetal, Universidad Politecnica de Valencia. Valencia. Spain link[276]

"L'Etat Actuel De L'Electroculture. Par M. E. Guarini. Verlag Der Revue Scientifique, Paris. 24 Seiten Mit 3 Abbildungen Gen. Preis 1 Fr." 1904. Zeitschrift Für Elektrochemie Und Angewandte Physikalische Chemie 10 (16): 264–264. doi:10.1002/bbpc.19040101608. link[277]

Detección de Leifsonia xyli subsp. xyli en Caña de Azúcar (Saccharum spp.), Saneamiento Mediante Técnicas Biotecnológicas. Dagoberto Guillen, Ricardo Hernández, Lisbet Rodríguez y Rafael Gómez. Campus Oriente, Univ. Autónoma del estado de Morelos. México. CETAS. Universidad de Cienfuegos, Cuba. Estación Experimental de la Caña de Azúcar (EPICA), Ranchuelo, VC, Cuba.

---

[272] http://rd.springer.com/chapter/10.1007/978-3-540-37843-3_11

[273] http://www.bio.ic.ac.uk/research/agold/goldsworthy.htm

[274] http://www.rcsb.org/pdb/101/motm.do?momID=51&evtc=Suggest&evta=Moleculeof%20the%20Month&evtl=TopBar

[275] http://www.thefreelibrary.com/Grow+healthier+crops%3A+the+art+%26+science+of+electroculture.-a0229227369

[276] http://irrec.ifas.ufl.edu/flcitrus/pdfs/short_course_and_workshop/citrus_flowering_97/Guardiola-Increasing_Citrus_Fruit_Size.pdf

[277] http://onlinelibrary.wiley.com/doi/10.1002/bbpc.19040101608/abstract

Instituto de Biotecnología de las Plantas (IBP), UCLV, Cuba link[278]

H

Hansen, Truls Lynne, "The northern lights-what are they?", Tromsø Geophysical Observatory, University of Tromsø.

Hassanein, W A, and A A Ali. 2013. "STUDY OF THE INFLUENCE OF ELECTRIC FIELD EXPOSURE ON SOME SOIL MICROBIAL ACTIVITIES." Egyptian Society For Biotechnology. Accessed May 22. link[279]

Häntzschel, Walter, "The influence of electricity on plant growth", Inventions and experiments - Volume II, W. Herlet, Leipzig 1906 (Ref)[280]

Henehan, Sean, Electric Tomatoes, Planta Jounal, June 1997 via Access Excellence link[281]

Hepler, Peter K. 2005. "Calcium: A Central Regulator of Plant Growth and Development." The Plant Cell Online 17 (8) (8–1): 2142–2155. doi:10.1105/tpc.105.032508. link[282]

Hodko, Dalibor. 2000. "Electrokinetic Remediation Prefield Test Methods."

Hormozi-Nejad, M. H., J. Mozafari, and F. Rakhshandehroo. 2010. "Elimination of Bean Common Mosaic Virus Using an Electrotherapy Technique." Journal of Plant Diseases and Protection (JPDP) 5 (117): 201–205. link[283]

Hull, George S. 1898. Electro-horticulture. New York: The Knickerbocker Press.

---

[278] http://www.smbb.com.mx/revista/Revista_2007_2/Leifsonia_Saccharum.pdf
[279] http://esbiotech.org/index.php/egyptian-journal-of-biotechnology/2004/177-vol-17/442-19-17-study-of-the-influence-of-electric-field-exposure-on-some-soil-microbial-activities
[280] http://de.m.wikipedia.org/wiki/Elektrokultur#
[281] http://www.accessexcellence.org/WN/SUA10/tomato697.php
[282] http://www.plantcell.org/content/17/8/2142
[283] http://www.ulmer-journals.de/ojs/index.php/jpdp/article/view/266

I

Ishikawa, Hideo, and Michael L. Evans. 1990. "Electrotropism of Maize Roots 1." Plant Physiology 94 (3) (November): 913–918.

Committee, I. (2012). Agriculture in the Arctic. link[284]

J

Jain, S. Mohan. 2011. Date Palm Biotechnology. Springer. link[285]

PHYSICAL METEOROLOGY John Clark Johnson. The Technology Press and John Wiley & Sons, Inc., 1954. via[286]

K

Plant Cell Biology by Dr. G. R. Kantharaj, M.Sc. (Bangalore University), Ph.D. (Indian Institute of Science), Reader (Retd.), Dept. of Botany, The National College, Visiting Professor, Bangalore University, Principal Scientist (Retd.), Genetic Engineering Lab, IAHS, BANGALORE, INDIA link[287]

L

Lamont, J. V. (1862). Der Erdstrom und der Zusammen desselben mit dem Erdmagnetismus. Leipzig und Muenchen: Leopold-Voss-Verlag.

Telluric Currents: The Natural Environment and Interactions with Man-Made Systems, Louis J. Lanzerotti, AT&T Bell Laboratories, Giovanni P. Gregori, Istituto Di Fisica Dell'Atmosfera, Rome

National Research Council. The Earth's Electrical Environment. Washington, DC: The National Academies Press, 1986.

Lemström K, Electricity in agriculture and horticulture. Electrician Publications, London, 1904

Lindgren, E. R., Brady, P. V., IN SITU ELECTROKINETIC CON-

---

[284] http://www.eoearth.org/view/article/149915/
[285] http://books.google.com/books?id=N3xf-80L-AQC
[286] http://jesseenterprises.net/amsci/1957/05/1957-05-fs.html
[287] http://plantcellbiology.masters.grkraj.org/html/Plant_Growth_And_Development4-Plant_Hormones-Gibberellins.htm

TROL OF MOISTURE AND NUTRIENTS IN UNSATURATED SOILS, Sandia National Laboratories, Albuquerque NM 87185, p4

Lippert, Bob. "Cation Exchange Capacity and Percent Base Saturation." link[288]

Nature, Volume 20, Edited by Sir Norman Lockyer. 1879, "Influence of Electricity on Vegetation" link[289]

Loghavi, Laleh, Sudhir K Sastry, and Ahmed E Yousef. 2008. "Effect of moderate electric field frequency on growth kinetics and metabolic activity of Lactobacillus acidophilus." Biotechnology progress 24 (1) (January–February): 148–153. doi:10.1021/bp070268v. link[290]

M

Jie, Ma, and Zhou Shengxue. 2012. "Effects of Low Direct Current Electric Field on the Growth and Metabolism of Bacillus Subtilis." Chinese Journal of Applied Chemistry 29 (4): 422–427. doi:10.3724/SP.J.1095.2012.00198. link[291]

Electrophysiology and Plant Responses to Biotic Stress, Massimo Maffei, Simone Bossi link[292]

McCaig, C. D., B. Song, and A. M. Rajnicek. 2009. "Electrical Dimensions in Cell Science." Journal of Cell Science 122 (23) (November 18): 4267–4276. doi:10.1242/jcs.023564. link[293]

"The Earth's Electricity," by James E. McDonald; SCIENTIFIC AMERICAN, April, 1953.

H.N. McLeod, Transactions of the New Zealand Institute, vol xxv, p.479, 1892

Miyake N.H., Taniguchi T.(1995). Ultrastructural changes of chloro-

[288] http://hubcap.clemson.edu/~blpprt/IL64.html
[289] http://books.google.com/books?id=L8MKAAAAYAAJ&lpg=PA587&ots=p6BNRMIfIf&dq=Grandeau%20and%20Leclerq&pg=PA587#v=onepage&q=Grandeau%20and%20Leclerq&f=false
[290] http://www.ncbi.nlm.nih.gov/pubmed/18184003
[291] http://yyhx.ciac.jl.cn/EN/abstract/article_12160.shtml
[292] http://link.springer.com/chapter/10.1007/978-3-540-37843-3_20
[293] http://europepmc.org/abstract/MED/19923270/reload=0;jsessionid=B7NCFc5JzDmjHLuXz4EM.26

plasts in peanut mesophyll protoplasts treated with electric fields. Jpn. J. Crop Sci. 64,131–138.

Morares, C. M. De, W. J. Lewis, P. W. Paré, H. T. Alborn, and J. H. Tumlinson. 1998. "Herbivore-infested Plants Selectively Attract Parasitoids." Nature 393 (6685) (June 11): 570–573. doi:10.1038/31219. link1[294] link2[295]

N

Norton, Patti, The Aurora Borealis and the Telegraph, Rainbow Riders Trading Post, 2008 link[296]

Niroumand, Hamed, Nazir, Ramli, Kassim, Khairul Anuar, The Performance of Electrochemical Remediation Technologies in Soil Mechanics, International Journal od Electrochemical Science 7 (2012) 5708-5715 link[297]

O

Okumura, T.; Muramoto, Y.; Shimizu, N.; , "Acceleration of plant growth by D.C. electric field," 2010 10th IEEE International Conference on Solid Dielectrics (ICSD), pp.1-4, 4-9 July 2010 doi: 10.1109/ICSD.2010.5568265 link[298]

Okumura, T, Y Muramoto, and N Shimizu. 2009. "Influence of Electric Field on Plant Weight." Electrical Insulation and Dielectric Phenomena, 2009. CEIDP '09. IEEE Conference On (October 18–21). doi:10.1109/CEIDP.2009.5377852. link[299]

Osborne, Daphné J.; McManus, Michael T. (2005). Hormones, signals and target cells in plant development. Cambridge University Press. p. 158. ISBN 978-0-521-33076-3.

Essay: Communications between plant cells, Overall, Robyn, Plants In Action, Edition #1, Copyright © Australian Society of Plant Sci-

---

[294]http://www.nature.com/nature/journal/v393/n6685/abs/393570a0.html
[295]http://naldc.nal.usda.gov/download/81/PDF
[296]http://www.rainbowriderstradingpost.com/article1.html
[297]http://www.electrochemsci.org/papers/vol7/7065708.pdf
[298]http://ieeexplore.ieee.org/stamp/stamp.jsp?tp=&arnumber=5568265&isnumber=5567194
[299]http://ieeexplore.ieee.org/xpl/login.jsp?tp=&arnumber=5377852

Bibliography 215

entists, New Zealand Society of Plant Biologists, and New Zealand Institute of Agricultural and Horticultural Science 1999 link[300]

P

Paré, Paul W., and James H. Tumlinson. 1999. "Plant Volatiles as a Defense Against Insect Herbivores." Plant Physiology 121 (2) (10-1): 325–332. doi:10.1104/pp.121.2.325. link[301].

Plowman, Amon B. 1904. "Electrotropism of Roots." The American Journal of Science XVII (97): 228.

Q

Luo, Qishi, Hui Wang, Xihui Zhang, and Yi Qian. 2005. "Effect of Direct Electric Current on the Cell Surface Properties of Phenol-Degrading Bacteria." Applied and Environmental Microbiology 71 (1) (January): 423–427. doi:10.1128/AEM.71.1.423-427.2005. link[302]

S

Saito, Mitsu - Letter to David Wechsler. 2012. "RE: What Are You up To?"

"THE ELECTRICAL PROCESS OF MILK PASTEURIZATION." Sally H. Stabler, Laboratories of Bacteriology and Chemical Hygiene at John Hopkins University, 1931. link[303]

Seifriz, William. 1929. "The Structure of Protoplasm." Biological Reviews 4 (1): 76–102. doi:10.1111/j.1469-185X.1929.tb00987.x. link[304]

Silverstone, Matthew, Blinded By Science, Lloyd's World Publishing, 2011, p.303 link[305]

Solly, E., Chapter Title: On the Influence of Galvanic Electricity On The Germination of Seeds, Report on the Fifteenth Meeting of the

---

[300] http://plantsinaction.science.uq.edu.au/edition1/?q=content/feature-essay-10-1-communication-between-plant-cells
[301] http://www.plantphysiol.org/content/121/2/325
[302] http://www.ncbi.nlm.nih.gov/pmc/articles/PMC544265/
[303] http://aje.oxfordjournals.org/content/14/2/433.full.pdf
[304] http://onlinelibrary.wiley.com/doi/10.1111/j.1469-185X.1929.tb00987.x/abstract
[305] http://www.blindedbyscience.co.uk/

British Society for the Advancement of Science Held in Cambridge June 1845, John Murray, Albermarle Street, London, 1846 ,p.69 link[306]

Experiments Which Show That the Earth Functions As an Electrostatic Machine by C. L. Stong, May 1957 link[307]

Suni, Sonja, and Martin Romantschuk. 2004. "Mobilisation of Bacteria in Soils by Electro-osmosis." FEMS Microbiol Ecol (July 1). link[308]

T

Takamura, Tsutomu. 2006. "Electrochemical Potential Around the Plant Root in Relation to Metabolism and Growth Acceleration." In Plant Electrophysiology, edited by Prof Dr Alexander G. Volkov, 341–374. Springer Berlin Heidelberg. link[309]

Source: TAIZ, L. and ZEIGER, E. 2002 and 2010: Plant Physiology, 3rd and 5th Edition. The Benjamin Cummings Publishing Company, Redwood City - California

Taiz L., Zeiger E., Sensitivity of various physiological processes to changes in water potential under various growing conditions, 2010, link[310]

Thomashow, Michael F. 1999. "PLANT COLD ACCLIMATION: Freezing Tolerance Genes and Regulatory Mechanisms." Annual review of plant physiology and plant molecular biology 50 (June): 571–599. doi:10.1146/annurev.arplant.50.1.571.

Tiqiang, Yang, Hou Jianhua, Su Enguang, Na Ri, and Guo Weisheng. 1999. "Effect of electric field treatment of oil sunflower seeds on

---

[306]http://books.google.com/books?id=LedJAAAAcAAJ&dq=davy%20barley%20turnips%20radishes%20electricity&pg=PR3#v=onepage&q=davy%20barley%20turnips%20radishes%20electricity&f=false
[307]http://laplace.ucv.cl/Cursos/TrabajoTitulo/ExperimentosBajoCosto/VanDerGraaf/VanDerGraaf02.html
[308]http://www.ncbi.nlm.nih.gov/pubmed/19712383
[309]http://link.springer.com/chapter/10.1007/978-3-540-37843-3_15
[310]http://www.tankonyvtar.hu/hu/tartalom/tamop425/0010_1A_Book_angol_01_novenyelettan/ch02.html

the growth under drought stress in seedling stage." Shengwu Wuli Xuebao 16 (4) (December): 780–784. link[311]

Adesemoye, A. O., H. A. Torbert, and J. W. Kloepper. 2009. "Plant Growth-Promoting Rhizobacteria Allow Reduced Application Rates of Chemical Fertilizers." Microbial Ecology 58 (4) (November 1): 921–929. doi:10.1007/s00248-009-9531-y. link[312]

Tuteja, Narendra, and Shilpi Mahajan. 2007. "Calcium Signaling Network in Plants." Plant Signaling & Behavior 2 (2): 79–85. link[313]

Truffault, George. 1935. "Electricity Controls Tree Growth." Popular Science, August. link[314] link[315]

U

Uman, Martin; Has Lightning Any Practical Use, 1996 link[316]

V

Volkov, Alexander G., and Courtney L. Brown. 2006. "Electrochemistry of Plant Life." In Plant Electrophysiology, edited by Alexander G. Volkov, 437–459. Berlin, Heidelberg: Springer Berlin Heidelberg. link[317]

Volkov, Alexander G., Applied Electrical Phenonema, #6, 1966, Nov-Dec. P 394 via Rex Research articles on Electroculture #2.

Volkov, Alexander G., Applied Electrical Phenonema, #6, 1966, Nov-Dec. P 394 via Rex Research articles on Electroculture #2.

Volkov, Alexander G., Plant Electrophysiology: Theory and Methods link[318] - p.254 via (Adey 1990)

---

[311] http://europepmc.org/abstract/CBA/342189
[312] http://link.springer.com/article/10.1007/s00248-009-9531-y
[313] http://www.ncbi.nlm.nih.gov/pmc/articles/PMC2633903/
[314] http://www.rexresearch.com/agro2/0agro1.htm#shokweed
[315] http://plantcellbiology.masters.grkraj.org/html/Plant_Growth_And_Development4-Plant_Hormones-Gibberellins.htm
[316] http://www.ira.usf.edu/cam/exhibitions/1998_12_McCollum/supplemental_didactics/20.Uman17.pdf
[317] http://rd.springer.com/chapter/10.1007/978-3-540-37843-3_19
[318] http://books.google.com/books?id=6a1_Gw8Tt10C&lpg=PA254&ots=ASCIRAjbKh&dq=Adey%201990%20volkov&pg=PA254#v=onepage&q=Adey%201990%20volkov&f=false

W

Wang, Dong, Jiancheng Song, and Tianhe Kang. 2011. "Electromotive Force in Electrochemical Modification of Mudstone." In Electromotive Force and Measurement in Several Systems, edited by Sadik Kara. InTech. link[319]

WangJinPeng, The Significant Conditions of Electric Field Treatment Effects on Drought Resistance of the Caragana Seeds, Inner Mongolia University link[320]

Wang, Ya-qin, and Ji-hong Wang. 2004. "Effect of Electric Fertilizer on Soil Properties." Chinese Geographical Science 14 (1) (March 1): 71–74. doi:10.1007/s11769-004-0011-5. link[321]

Interview with Doug Weatherbee of Soildoctor.org. 2011. Podcast. 2 vols. Interview with Doug Weatherbee. link[322]

Wawrecki, Wojciech, and Beata Zagórska-Marek. 2007. "Influence of a Weak DC Electric Field on Root Meristem Architecture." Annals of Botany 100 (4) (10–1): 791–796. doi:10.1093/aob/mcm164. link[323]

Wayne, Randy. 1994. "The Excitability of Plant Cells: With a Special Emphasis on Characean Internodal Cells." The Botanical Review 60 (3) (July 1): 265–367. doi:10.1007/BF02960261. link[324]

Wieczorek, S., H. Weigand, and C. Marb. "Applying Electrokinetic Phenonema to the Remediation of Inorganic Contaminants in the Unsaturated Zone: From Lab- to Pilot-scale Experiments". Bavarian Environmental Protection Agency. link[325]

---

[319] http://www.intechopen.com/books/electromotive-force-and-measurement-in-several-systems/electromotive-force-in-electrochemical-modification-of-mudstone
[320] http://www.agrpaper.com/the-significant-conditions-of-electric-field-treatment-effects-on-drought-resistance-of-the-caragana-seeds.htm
[321] http://link.springer.com/article/10.1007/s11769-004-0011-5
[322] http://permaculturenews.org/2011/01/28/sustainable-world-radio-interview-with-doug-weatherbee-life-within-the-soil-part-i/
[323] http://aob.oxfordjournals.org/content/100/4/791
[324] http://link.springer.com/article/10.1007/BF02960261
[325] http://www.bodenkunde2.uni-freiburg.de/eurosoil/abstracts/id618_Wieczorek_full.pdf

Y

Adam Yare, Forum posting link[326]

Young, Stephen. 1997. "Growing in Electric Fields." New Scientist, 8–23. link[327]

Z

Zvitov, R., C. Zohar-Perez, and A. Nussinovitch. 2004. "Short-Duration Low-Direct-Current Electrical Field Treatment Is a Practical Tool for Considerably Reducing Counts of Gram-Negative Bacteria Entrapped in Gel Beads." Applied and Environmental Microbiology 70 (6) (6–1): 3781–3784. doi:10.1128/AEM.70.6.3781-3784.2004. link[328]

MISC

biology-online.org[329]

University of Queensland Australia, School of Information Technology and Electrical Engineering, user "nic", "Basics of Gene Expression"

Web page: Chapter 4, The University of British Columbia Geophysical inversion facility link[330]

Anon. 1892. "Actinism." The Electrician 29 (June 3): 110.

Anon. 1935. "Electricity Controls Tree Growth." Popular Science, August.

US Patent #690151[331]

Anon. 1985. "ELECTRICITY MAY PLAY ROLE IN PLANT GROWTH."

---

[326] http://science.blurtit.com/13267/does-lightning-really-help-plants
[327] http://www.newscientist.com/article/mg15520965.000-growing-in-electric-fields.html
[328] http://aem.asm.org/content/70/6/3781
[329] http://www.biology-online.org/11/10_growth_and_plant_hormones.htm
[330] http://www.eos.ubc.ca/ubcgif/iag/foundations/properties/resistivity.htm
[331] http://www.google.com/patents/US690151

The New York Times, April 9, sec. Science. link[332]

Gardeners Chronicle and new horticulturist, April 9, 1904, p.227 link[333]

How Plants Grow in Response to Their Environment. McGraw-Hill Online Learning Centerlink [334]

Wikipedia Contributors, "Appropriate Technology." Wikipedia, the Free Encyclopedia link[335]

Wikipedia Contributors, "Calcium Signaling." Wikipedia, the Free Encyclopedia link[336]

Wikipedia: Chlorosis link[337]

Wikipedia: Electrolyte link[338]

Wikipedia Contributors, "Electrotropism," Wikipedia, The Free Encyclopedia link[339]

Wikipedia contributors. 2012. "History of Fertilizer." Wikipedia, the Free Encyclopedia. Wikimedia Foundation, Inc. link[340]

Wikipedia contributors. 2012. "Kaolinite." Wikipedia, the Free Encyclopedia. Wikimedia Foundation, Inc. link[341]

Wikipedia: Plant Hormone link[342]

Wikipedia Contributors, "Resting Potential," Wikipedia, The Free Encyclopedia link[343]

---

[332] http://www.nytimes.com/1985/04/09/science/electricity-may-play-role-in-plant-growth.html
[333] http://books.google.com/books?id=UthIAAAAYAAJ&lpg=PA227&ots=EHAH6W4UgL&dq=norway%20electroculture&pg=PA227#v=onepage&q=norway%20electroculture&f=false
[334] http://highered.mcgraw-hill.com/sites/0073031208/student_view0/chapter41/elearning_sessions.html
[335] http://en.wikipedia.org/w/index.php?title=Appropriate_technology
[336] http://en.wikipedia.org/w/index.php?title=Calcium_signaling
[337] https://en.wikipedia.org/wiki/Chlorosis
[338] http://en.wikipedia.org/wiki/Electrolyte
[339] http://en.wikipedia.org/wiki/Electrotropism
[340] http://en.wikipedia.org/w/index.php?title=History_of_fertilizer&oldid=497166883
[341] http://en.wikipedia.org/w/index.php?title=Kaolinite&oldid=506595887
[342] http://en.wikipedia.org/wiki/Plant_hormone
[343] http://en.wikipedia.org/w/index.php?title=Resting_potential

Bibliography

Wikipedia Contributors, "Soil pH." Wikipedia, the Free Encyclopedia. link[344]

Wikipedia Contributors, "Standard Electrode Potential." Wikipedia, the Free Encyclopedia. link[345]

Wikipedia contributors. 2012. "Systemic Acquired Resistance." Wikipedia, the Free Encyclopedia. Wikimedia Foundation, Inc. link[346]

Wikipedia Contributors, "Telluric_current," Wikipedia, The Free Encyclopedia link[347]

Yahoo - Electroculture Advantages. link[348]

"Explain Action Potential and Resting Potential- All or None Rule?" 2013. Accessed February 6. link[349]

"Why Do Roots Need Oxygen?" 2013. Accessed February 5. link[350]

Web Page: Plants and the Environment: Tropisms, Circadian Rhythms and More; Krempels, Dana M., University of Miami, Department of Biology link[351].

---

[344] http://en.wikipedia.org/wiki/Soil_pH
[345] http://en.wikipedia.org/wiki/Standard_electrode_potential_%28data_page%29
[346] http://en.wikipedia.org/wiki/Systemic_acquired_resistance
[347] http://en.wikipedia.org/wiki/Telluric_current
[348] http://uk.answers.yahoo.com/question/index?qid=20080617061035AAJ4M8w
[349] http://answers.yahoo.com/question/index?qid=20101006151703AAHsOec
[350] http://answers.yahoo.com/question/index?qid=20080919164602AA4lvc6
[351] http://www.bio.miami.edu/dana/226/226F08_21.html

Acknowledgments

I would like to especially thank my family and friends who have given me the encouragement along the way to keep going.

Furthermore, I would like to give a hearty thanks to everyone who has helped me put this book together including:

- Main illustrator, William Perry (@moleculefarm[352]) and Vicki Bernal who helped with the latest cover design concept
- Proofreader-editors: Joelle Schoenherr, Eberly Barnes, Donna Daniels, Jason Machin, Sheldon Hoffman, everyone who helped with working on the title, subtitle and critique: Avery Kravitz, Johnathan Brown, Russ Hamm, Angel Gonzalez, James Schiller, Bryce Hobbs, Edward Bent, Mike Toppen, Kukunemo (Gina) Sensi, Shane Bland, Eldon Diment, Michael Bray, Nicole White, Lewis Conley, Denzil Gouws, Giancarlo Quadri
- All of the researchers I have referenced in the bibliography - for their hard work and research efforts
- Joshua Dorkin for your valued knowledge, experience, and encouragement along the way, Weber & Lang Pharis for their close experimental collaboration and photo contributions, and lastly, everyone who has purchased this book while it was in varying stages of development!

---

[352]https://twitter.com/moleculefarm

Printed in Great Britain
by Amazon